As a former teacher and now a homeschooling mom, I have seen very few resources that give parents such valuable tools to enrich their teaching styles and create success at home. Tamara gives parents all the benefits of an education degree and her years of creative teaching experience in a short, easy-to-read format. ***Homeschooling with TLC in the Elementary Grades*** *will change every parent's method of teaching and make learning at home fun and effective!*

~Shannon Dardaman
certified teacher & home educator

Homeschooling with TLC in the Elementary Grades *contains great practical advice for the homeschooling parent. The information Tamara has included will help me become a better home educator by placing creativity and scheduling ideas at my fingertips. From the reading concepts and outline of math manipulatives and games to the creative writing and spelling suggestions, it is a treasure trove of information. It has really encouraged me. I am excited about our school year!*

~Terry Pierce
home educator & founder of
HEARTHSTONES homeschool group

Homeschooling with TLC in the Elementary Grades *has been the most practical and least intimidating homeschooling book I have read in my first year of homeschooling. It included samples of charts, lesson plans, and websites, which I found extremely helpful. I recommend this book to all homeschooling parents. It is definitely a must read!*

~Judy Savage
beginning home educator

Homeschooling with TLC

in the Elementary Grades

A Practical Guide with Fun and Effective Teaching Tips

Tamara L. Chilver

TLC
EDITIONS
Fort Myers, Florida

Homeschooling with TLC

in the Elementary Grades

Information on Tamara L. Chilver's ministries and ordering books can be found on-line at *www.teachingwithtlc.com.*
Illustrations used with permission from *The Official Book of Homeschooling Cartoons* by Todd Wilson at *www.familymanweb.com*.

While the author has made every effort to provide accurate Internet addresses at the time of publication, the author is not responsible for errors or changes that occur after publication.

Library of Congress Control Number: 2007928483

ISBN: 978-0-9796313-0-6

Published by TLC Editions
Fort Myers, FL

A special thanks to:
Haleigh Katwaroo and Marie Mosley, APR- editing

DEDICATION

♥♥♥

*The Lord bless you and keep you;
the Lord make His face shine upon you
and be gracious to you; the Lord turn His
face to you and give you peace.*

~ *Numbers 6:24-26*

This book is dedicated to all the parents who homeschool their children. Homeschooling is a selfless commitment that brings a lifetime of rewards. My best wishes to you and your family during your homeschool journey.

After Johnson spoke, they knew that they had been topped

Homeschooling with TLC in the Elementary Grades is designed for children who are homeschooled. If your child is attending school and in a classroom setting, refer to ***Tutoring Your Elementary Child with TLC*** for more specific ideas on educating your child.

CONTENTS

♥♥♥

ACKNOWLEDGEMENTS

God has blessed me with incredible mentors in my life of education. They all have helped me become the teacher that I am.

Jason Chilver- Without my husband's persevering love and steadfast support, homeschooling would not be possible. I truly love him more with each passing day, and I am privileged to be his wife.

Helen Crowell- My grandmother made my dream of becoming an elementary teacher a reality by financially supporting me through college. She also taught me unconditional love. I could always count on her words of encouragement. Even though she has gone to be with the Lord,I know she is still cheering me on.

Dr. Gloria Houston- My college professor taught me how to teach outside the box. Her unique teaching methods and strategies were an eye-opening experience. She taught me to break away from textbooks and venture into a world of exploration.

Margie Eddings- Unlike most people, my favorite teacher is not from grade school or high school. I did not meet her until my internship in college. I was in awe of Margie's teaching style from the first day I walked into her classroom. She taught me how to teach creatively and actively engage the students. She invented the meaning of a fun, learning environment!

Lynn Wade- My principal during my years as an elementary teacher valued me as a professional and inspired me to strive for greatness, moving beyond merely acceptable results.

Carol Melious- God knew what He was doing when he put this loving woman in my life as my co-teacher. She taught me how to nurture a child's learning and instill a desire for more.

Jennifer Otte- My dear friend encouraged me to cross over into the homeschooling world. She guided the way in uncharted territory, while providing me with much needed confidence.

Conley, Colton, and Coen Chilver- My beautiful children make homeschooling the best educational experience of my life!

INTRODUCTION

♥♥

If you truly want to bless others in your life, you must seek out those experiences that keep you motivated and inspired and then share them.

~ Thomas Kinkade

I sincerely believe God has given me a diverse background in elementary education and has planted a desire in my heart to serve Him by assisting parents who homeschool their children. My bachelor's degree is in elementary education, and my master's degree is in elementary curriculum. I am blessed to be the mother of three boys. Before entering the homeschooling world several years ago, I was an elementary teacher, a curriculum coordinator, and a private tutor.

Many people come to me seeking advice during their homeschooling journeys. They have chosen their curriculum and are filled with excitement, yet they feel a little lost. There are still many questions to be answered that curriculum programs alone do not cover. First, I will address these questions and reveal the tools of the trade. Second, I will discuss a common fear of homeschooling parents, which is feeling unqualified to teach, while providing you with the confidence you need to successfully educate your child at home.

I wrote this guide to help and encourage homeschooling parents. I make many references to different products and resources, but my purpose is not to solely recommend these for your child. You may have researched and purchased what you feel are the best products for your child's specific needs. I am offering additional ideas to supplement your chosen method of instruction. Most of the products in this book are available through links at *www.teachingwithtlc.com.*

I recommend you read the chapters of this book in order since many skills set the foundation for proceeding chapters. All subjects are interrelated. I separated the core subjects for this book's purpose, but many methods can overlap into several subject areas. I am thrilled to share my experiences and passion for learning with you, so let's get started!

Moments after the birth of Johnson baby #5

CHAPTER 1

♥♥

GETTING TO KNOW YOUR CHILD

No one has yet realized the wealth of sympathy, the kindness, and generosity hidden in the soul of a child. The effort of every true education should be to unlock that treasure.

~Emma Goldman

You think you know your child, right? I thought I did, too. I have found that there are several essential steps in knowing and meeting your child's needs. These should be your first priority in creating the best learning environment for your child.

Determine your child's learning style.

Learning styles are different ways that we as individuals perceive and process information. Recognizing and appreciating learning styles can help you identify the strengths of your child's learning. There are three basic modalities: visual, auditory, and kinesthetic. Visual learners tend to learn by watching and looking at pictures; auditory learners by hearing and listening; and kinesthetic learners through moving, doing, and touching.

Unfortunately, the majority of educators teach primarily through visual methods by using posters, overheads, textbooks, and chalkboards.

In addition, many educators will teach the way they best learn without realizing they are doing it.

I taught my oldest son for several years mostly through a visual method because I falsely assumed he learns the same way I do. I was also conditioned in this way of teaching from my classroom experiences. I should have known better. I studied learning styles in college, yet I never actually tested my son. Boy, did I get a surprise when I tested him! He was predominantly kinesthetic, with some auditory tendencies. I had been teaching him outside of his most natural learning style for years.

The lesson here is not to assume you know your child's learning style. Do your research. Cynthia Tobias' *The Way They Learn* provides parents with a fascinating insight into how people learn and how we can use that information to profitably understand our children better.

Try to incorporate all learning styles in your lessons, especially if you are teaching more than one child. If your child is learning something new or begins to struggle with a concept, teach primarily using his dominant learning style to help him grasp the concept easier.

Discover your child's love language.

Did you know your child has a primary language of love? This is the way he understands your love best. *The Five Love Languages of Children* by Gary Chapman and Ross Campbell will introduce you to all of these love languages: quality time, words of affirmation, gifts, acts of service, and physical touch. This book will help you determine the primary language in which your child hears your love, and it will teach you how you can effectively meet his deepest emotional needs. Your child will reach his highest motivation and success levels in learning when you understand his love language.

Now you will know the best way to teach your child and motivate your child, but...

Do not forget discipline.

One of the most frequent comments I get from people who do not homeschool their children is, "I could never teach my own children because they would not listen to me."

I have to carefully refrain from speaking what I am thinking, which is that is a discipline problem, not a teaching issue. Many parents often feel like they cannot teach their own child. They feel pressured to pay hundreds or thousands of dollars per year for tutoring services or schooling because they falsely assume their child will not listen to them. If this is your situation, you may discover the issue is in discipline.

We must have our children obey us as parents whether we homeschool our children or send them to school. The foundation of respect and obedience is essential for any home. Submission to parental authority prepares our children to submit to God. As a mother, I make it a priority to read books, attend seminars and workshops, and seek advice from friends and family on discipline. It is something we must continually work on as parents.

My favorite discipline books that I refer to often are *The New Dare to Discipline* by Dr. James Dobson and *Creative Correction* by Lisa Whelchel. I recommend purchasing a book on children's discipline because your child is constantly growing and entering new phases, and you may need to refer to it many times for fresh ideas and advice.

Create an atmosphere for learning.

Establish a relaxed setting that is conducive to learning. Students are often easily distracted. Make sure you are in a relatively quiet area with good light. Clear the table of other materials, so your child can focus on the subject at hand. Sit next to your child, not across the table from him, to effectively facilitate learning.

Open communication is vital when teaching your child. Be an active listener. Let your child know what he says is important. Ask questions and restate his ideas in your own words to make sure you understand his answers.

Explain the assignment to your child slowly, and give him one direction at a time. Complete the first problem or some examples together when beginning an assignment. Be patient and give your child plenty of time to answer. Silence can mean he is organizing what he wants to say or write.

Encourage your child to do his own thinking and work independently on material that comes easily. Provide suggestions and information sources to help your child if he does not know the answer. Your ultimate goal is to have your child working independently in every subject area.

Now that we have laid a solid foundation for the best learning environment for your child, let's move on to curriculum choices.

Cut down in the prime of his life, Steve suddenly found himself between a half-off book sale and 800 homeschooling moms.

CHAPTER 2

♥♥

CHOOSING YOUR CURRICULUM

Education is not preparation for life;
education is life itself.

~John Dewey

Choosing your curriculum can be one of the most stressful parts of homeschooling. As parents, we want the absolute best for our children, but it can often be an overwhelming experience trying to determine which curriculum meets our children's needs.

If you are having a difficult time selecting a curriculum, I encourage you to read Cathy Duffy's *100 Top Picks for Homeschool Curriculum.* Cathy is a curriculum specialist who offers her "top picks" from each subject area and walks her readers through the process of figuring out their philosophy of education, learning styles, and goal setting. Here are some additional steps you can take to make the selection process easier.

Make a list and refine it twice.

Create a list of attainable goals for the school year. There are academic, physical, work study, and character development goals that you can set for your child. Homeschooling allows the whole child to be taught in every aspect of his life, not solely academically.

I recommend using your state's scope (what will be taught) and sequence (when it will be taught) as a reference for setting your academic goals. Be concise and realistic. There is no need to try to teach ten subjects in one year. Concentrate primarily on the core subjects: reading, writing, math, and social studies/science.

When I first started homeschooling, I would rush through the school day and try to accomplish far too much. This was a habit I had incurred from teaching elementary school. I was so used to my students leaving me at the end of the school year that I would race through the curriculum to reach my goals. I knew I only had ten short months to cover everything I wanted and to make an impression that would hopefully last a lifetime.

I have broken that habit over the years. I now have a three-year plan, and I recommend you start one, too. This will enable you to become more relaxed with your teaching goals. On your three-year plan, write down everything you would like your child to learn. This method is particularly helpful for electives, such as: foreign language, drama, music, art, and sports. If your child's performance does not meet your objectives or you do not have time to cover a concept you had planned for that particular school year, simply write it on the following year's list of goals. The pressure is now off!

I have included two sample lesson plans on p. 19-20. These are what I used when I homeschooled my oldest son. These samples are very general. I was more specific on my copies by including page numbers, the names of the books we read and games we played, and information about our unit studies in science/social studies. I will discuss in detail the core subjects in this book and provide you with an ample amount of ideas for each. There is no "ideal" lesson plan since every child is unique. You can adapt these sample lesson plans to meet your child's needs by adding or deleting areas of interest.

My family's school time begins with the Pledge of Allegiance, calendar skills (review days, dates, and months for the young ones), devotions, and prayers. It is a blessing to be able to pray and do devotions together as a family each morning instead of rushing out the door. This is truly one advantage of homeschooling.

Notice how Friday is a relaxed day. I try to leave open a large amount of time for field trips and support group activities. It is also nice to have extra time to concentrate on skills that need additional practice.

I left a block of time open in the elective section. You can pick additional goals for the school year to address here. For example, if your child takes lessons for a musical instrument, write "practice instrument" in that block of space for each day.

PRIMARY LESSON PLAN

	MORNING ACTIVITIES	READING	LANGUAGE ARTS	MATH	SOCIAL STUDIES/ SCIENCE	ELECTIVE
MON	PLEDGE CALENDER DEVOTIONS PRAYERS READ ALOUD	PHONICS LESSON PHONICS GAME INDEPENDENT READING	HANDWRITING SPELLING WRITING	MATH LESSON	SOCIAL STUDIES/ SCIENCE	
TUE	PLEDGE CALENDER DEVOTIONS PRAYERS READ ALOUD	PHONICS LESSON INDEPENDENT READING	HANDWRITING SPELLING WRITING	MATH LESSON MATH GAME	SOCIAL STUDIES/ SCIENCE	
WED	PLEDGE CALENDER DEVOTIONS PRAYERS READ ALOUD	PHONICS LESSON PHONICS GAME INDEPENDENT READING	HANDWRITING SPELLING WRITING	MATH LESSON	SOCIAL STUDIES/ SCIENCE	
THU	PLEDGE CALENDER DEVOTIONS PRAYERS READ ALOUD	PHONICS LESSON INDEPENDENT READING	HANDWRITING SPELLING TEST WRITING	MATH LESSON MATH GAME	CURRENT EVENTS	
FRI	PLEDGE CALENDER DEVOTIONS PRAYERS READ ALOUD	INDEPENDENT READING	COMPUTER	ART	HOMESCHOOL SUPPORT GROUP/ FIELD TRIP	

UPPER ELEMENTARY LESSON PLAN

	MORNING ACTIVITIES	READING	LANGUAGE ARTS	MATH	SOCIAL STUDIES/ SCIENCE	ELECTIVE
MON	PLEDGE DEVOTIONS PRAYERS READ ALOUD	INDEPENDENT READING	SPELLING GRAMMAR WRITING	MATH LESSON	SOCIAL STUDIES/ SCIENCE	
TUE	PLEDGE DEVOTIONS PRAYERS READ ALOUD	INDEPENDENT READING	SPELLING GRAMMAR WRITING	MATH LESSON	SOCIAL STUDIES/ SCIENCE	
WED	PLEDGE DEVOTIONS PRAYERS READ ALOUD	INDEPENDENT READING	SPELLING READING COMPREHENSION WRITING	MATH LESSON	SOCIAL STUDIES/ SCIENCE	
THU	PLEDGE DEVOTIONS PRAYERS READ ALOUD	INDEPENDENT READING	SPELLING TEST WRITING- FINAL COPY	MATH LESSON MATH GAME	CURRENT EVENTS	
FRI	PLEDGE DEVOTIONS PRAYERS READ ALOUD	INDEPENDENT READING	COMPUTER	ART	HOMESCHOOL SUPPORT GROUP/ FIELD TRIP	

You may notice the upper elementary lesson plan looks like it has fewer assignments. These grades require more time to complete each task. For instance, I assign a larger allotment of time for independent reading and more math problems for older children than for younger children.

Get your needs met.

Search for a curriculum that meets your specifications. Make sure it addresses your objectives for your child, and it is user-friendly. Some curriculums require the parent to read a lot of information in teacher guides and gather plenty of materials before teaching. These would work for some parents, but others may have limited planning time.

Take into consideration the length of your school day. Be careful not to choose a curriculum that overworks your child. I recommend not exceeding five hours of school per day. Follow your state's guidelines for the minimum number of hours of schooling required per year. Remember to include the hours you spend educating your child that fall outside your school hours, such as learning activities and field trips during weekends and summertime. There is really no need for homework since its purpose is to reinforce lessons taught in school and to establish a sense of responsibility, which can be addressed in your child's homeschool day.

Do not be consumed with comparing the hours in your school day to a classroom setting. I can teach my children at home in half the time that is required in a classroom. It is not the quantity of time but the quality of education that counts. Thirty minutes of active learning is equivalent to several hours of passive learning.

Try to keep your child's afternoons open. Let your child be a kid! Your child will naturally pursue his own interests during these unscheduled downtimes. Just make sure the television is turned off.

There is no such thing as perfect.

Try to change your mindset from finding the perfect curriculum to finding a curriculum that meets the majority of your child's needs. I often see parents frantically shopping for one program that fulfills all their expectations. It is rare to find a parent who is completely satisfied. There will always be something to improve on or that can be changed. Do not let this discourage you. My master's degree is in elementary curriculum, and I have attended curriculum fairs for years. I have searched high and low, and there is not one "perfect" curriculum.

It's okay to mix-and-match. Do not be afraid of combining some programs to address each other's weaknesses. For example, one publisher may have an excellent reading curriculum while another publisher may have a fantastic writing curriculum. I have even done this in one particular subject area. I happened to like a phonics program and a reading comprehension program that were from two separate publishers. I combined the strengths of both without creating extra work.

You do not have to cover the entire curriculum.

Many parents feel a compulsive need to complete every assignment on every page in every book. I'll let you in on a secret; classroom teachers never finish the entire book either. Publishing companies always provide more than what is needed. If you want to complete the curriculum, but the school year has ended, insert a bookmark and pick up where you left off when school resumes.

Many parents struggle with this, and I must admit I was one of them. There was even a school year when my oldest son only made it through half of a math book because he was struggling with certain concepts. We continued using the same book the following school year. Do not rush your child to get through the book. Teach for mastery.

Learn to pick and choose. Again, you do not need to cover everything in the teacher's guides and lesson plans. It is alright to skip pages or even chapters. Maybe you would rather spend extra time on something else, or your child has already mastered those concepts. One quick way to assess if your child already knows the content is to have your child complete the chapter test. If your child knows the material, move on.

Stand on solid ground.

Make sure your lessons do not contradict the Word of God, which should be the foundation of your homeschool curriculum. Always look carefully over your books, and omit anything that conflicts with your beliefs when teaching. Whenever I use science and social studies books that make references to evolution, we simply skip over those pages. I do not recommend avoiding these books altogether because many have fabulous illustrations and information. Just use your discretion. This applies to videos and DVDs as well.

Go shopping.

Yes, you read this correctly. Shopping is an outstanding way to learn about different curriculums. Once a year, try to attend a local curriculum fair or a state convention, also known as "homeschool heaven," to keep up-to-date on new curriculums and revisions. There is no comparison to actually opening the books and looking through them. I can usually tell in a matter of minutes if a program will work for my family.

Ask around and do some research on-line before shopping. I enjoy discussing with fellow home educators what curriculums they are using and how they like them. Some of the best ideas I have used in my own home have been from other homeschooling mothers. Parents are honest when sharing the pros and cons. This can save you time and money when looking around.

Have a plan when you are going curriculum shopping. Do not try to decide on every subject area in one day. This will quickly overwhelm you. Try to narrow your search to just a few subject areas each time you attend these functions. Pick up free literature and material for future curriculum ideas.

Make sure your child likes the curriculum. I have taken my children shopping with me a few times to make the final decision. Also, make sure you like teaching the curriculum. Enthusiasm is contagious, so use it to your advantage.

A perk of attending curriculum fairs and conventions is there are often no shipping charges on most products. If you shop on-line or through a catalog, you take a risk on paying double shipping fees if you need to return something you are not content with. My favorite part of attending these functions is the inspiration I receive from being among others who share my desire to homeschool.

Make learning fun!

There will be a constant theme in this book- the process of learning should be exciting! Sometimes my younger children get sad when I do not have school on Saturdays. Even my oldest son does not want to take a summer break because he likes school days better. Why are my children like this? Because we make learning fun!

Do not put too much academic pressure on your child. Include game time and encourage creativity during your learning time together. Give your child choices, and use his interests to help guide your instructional time. If your child is fascinated with dinosaurs, have him read books and write stories about dinosaurs. The way you teach makes a world of difference!

The Homeschooling Library

CHAPTER 3

♥♥

RELIABLE READING METHODS

Education is not the filling of a pail
but the lighting of a fire.

~ William Butler Yeats

Reading is the most important subject because it overlaps into all subject areas. A strong foundation in reading will lead to success in other subjects. Learning to read is developmental. Some children need a lot of variety and repetition, while others seem to almost teach themselves. Take your time and progress at your child's own pace. Most importantly, do not rush to keep your child on "grade level." Children can catch up on years of reading in a matter of months. Regardless of what level your child has attained, here are some ideas you can add to any curriculum program.

Reading Instructional Time

There are three major components to making your reading instructional time the most effective. In the primary years, read aloud to your child, use a strong phonics program that includes hands-on activities, and have independent reading time. In the upper elementary grades, read aloud to your child, reinforce reading comprehension skills, and have independent reading time.

It is a great idea to teach reading as your first subject each day. Children's attention spans are usually the greatest in the morning because they have recently eaten, and their activity level is the lowest. Pick a relaxed place in your home for reading, such as a comfortable couch.

Begin reading time by reading aloud one or two picture books to a young child or a chapter from a book to an older child. You might be surprised to know older elementary children enjoy being read to just as much as younger children. Reading aloud models the stressing of syllables and accents in the pronunciation of words, and it teaches reading comprehension and listening skills. The rule of thumb is to always read aloud a little above your child's reading level. This ensures he is learning new vocabulary while you are paving the way for his reading journey.

To assess comprehension skills for books you read aloud and books read independently, ask the following questions.

Reading Comprehension Questions

(1) Where and when does the story take place?
(2) Who are the main characters?
(3) Who is your favorite character? Why?
(4) Which illustration do you like best?
(5) Which part of the story do you like best? Why?
(6) How do you feel about the end of the story?
(7) Do you think others would like to read this book?

These are the basic literary elements in a story.

Story Elements

Setting- when and where the story takes place
Main Characters- their appearance and personality traits
Plot- the problem the characters face and how they solve it
Conclusion- how the story ends

You can have your child complete graphic organizers to identify the elements of the story and the theme or moral of the story. There are a variety of graphic organizers you can use. Two of my favorites for analyzing a story are the "Story Star" and "Story Flower" because they allow the child to label the story in a simple, visual way. These two types of diagrams can be used to describe the elements of a story by using the five Ws: What, Who, Why, When, and Where.

Five Ws

What happened?
Who was there?
Why did it happen?
When did it happen?
Where did it happen?

For the Story Star, draw a very large five-pronged star. In the middle of the star, write the title of the book. Write in each prong of the star: What, Who, Why, When, and Where. For the Story Flower, use the same concept by writing the title of the book in a large circle. Label the five big petals with the five Ws around the circle. You can also use these graphic organizers when brainstorming during creative writing.

There are many terrific reading programs available. When choosing the program that best meets your young child's needs, make sure it has a strong foundation of phonics. Research shows using phonics sounds to read words works better than memorizing phonics rules. Just tell your child the sounds while reading. Do not focus on the rules.

My favorite phonics program, *Explode the Code* by Educators Publishing Service, is one of the most traditional and inexpensive ways to teach your child the sounds letters make. In this back-to-basics approach to learning phonics, a variety of exercises provide experience recognizing and combining sounds in order to read words, phrases, and sentences, as well as to build vocabulary. The pages are in black and white, which cause fewer visual distractions. I prefer using only books 1, 2, and 3. It never hurts to tape a couple of dollar bills to the back of the book for motivation.

I also use A Beka's *Handbook for Reading*, which provides practice lists for reading letter sounds. You can use these two recommendations as your main phonics program, or you can supplement your chosen program with these wonderful resources.

One reading program I often hear homeschool parents rave about is the Direct Instructional System for Teaching and Remediation (DISTAR). This highly acclaimed program shows parents how to teach their children to read with the manual *Teach Your Child to Read in 100 Easy Lessons* by SRA/McGraw-Hill Publishing. It provides an effective and economical way (the book is even available in public libraries) for teaching reading. Twenty minutes a day is all you need, and your child could be reading on a solid second-grade level within one hundred teaching days.

I have met many home educators who have had much success with *Hooked on Phonics*, an award-winning program that uses proven learning methods to provide beginning readers with a strong foundation in phonics and reading. With its step-by-step approach, children learn about letters and sounds and how to put them together to form words. This program includes a variety of multi-sensory tools that appeal to visual, auditory, and kinesthetic learners.

Your phonics instructional time should also include hands-on activities. Here are some hands-on games I have used to teach phonics: Alphabet Bingo by Trend Enterprises, Sight Word Bingo by Learning Resources, Phonics Board Games by Learning Resources, LeapFrog's Phonics Library, and Go-Fish for Letters by University Games Corporation. Similar games with the same educational concepts are manufactured by different companies. Make a habit of playing a phonics game at least every other day in the primary grades.

When your child has mastered letter sounds, he may be ready to learn to read independently. Some easy primers for beginning readers are *Bob Books* by Scholastic, *Now I'm Reading!* by Innovative Kids, and *Reader's Clubhouse* by Barron's Educational Series. These are usually available in libraries. You will need to follow the series you choose in order because the difficulty gradually increases.

For children who have mastered the basics of phonics, use Sylvan's Book Adventure (see p. 32) to select independent reading books on your child's level. Substitute your phonics instructional time for reading comprehension activities. I prefer using the quizzes on-line from Book Adventure and A Beka's Read and Think sheets to assess comprehension.

Reading Strategies

I have used these strategies to teach numerous children how to read. You can easily incorporate these into your reading instructional time to effectively engage your child in the reading process.

- **Read aloud-** Always read the book aloud first to the beginning reader. This way any new vocabulary words can be reviewed to help the child grasp the meaning of the story. Beginning readers are primarily focused on decoding the sounds and not comprehension. This is why reading aloud is so imperative.

- **Echo reading-** The parent reads and the child mimics the parent. This is super for beginning readers who need to learn to read with expression.

- **Cloze reading-** The parent reads and randomly stops, so the child has to read the next word. The parent continues to read and stop again.

- **Word train-** The parent reads a word, and the child reads the next word.

- **Flip-flop reading-** The parent reads a sentence, and the child reads a sentence. As the child reads more fluently, the parent reads a paragraph, and the child reads a paragraph. Slowly progress to the parent reads a page, and the child reads a page. This responsive reading technique can continue well into the middle school years. It is a quick way to assess a child's reading ability, and it keeps the child actively involved.

- **Stop-and-go reading-** The parent and the child take turns reading after commas *and* punctuation marks at the end of the sentences. This is great for reading with older children. It really keeps them on their toes.

- **Choral reading-** The parent and the child read together simultaneously.

- **Buddy-up-** Children enjoy reading to each other. Either a younger child can read with an older child guiding and correcting, or children of all levels can take turns doing flip-flop reading. Parents, be creative with this one. This is their favorite! They can read under a table, in a tent with flashlights, or outside under a tree.

  For parents who have more than one child, this is great to do when something interrupts your teaching time, and you do not want to stop school. Research shows older children benefit from being in a leadership role, and younger children benefit from the example of an older child.

- **Stump the parent-** This is wonderful for listening skills. While the parent reads aloud a page or two from a chapter book, the child thinks of a really good question to stump the parent. You will be surprised how well they can stump you, and they love it when they do!

- **Visual imagery-** The child draws the setting and characters in the story as the parent reads aloud. This is fantastic for chapter books with few illustrations. It helps children focus on details, which is also terrific for their listening skills.

- **D.E.A.R. time-** Drop Everything And Read is a silent reading time for everyone, including the parent, to read independently for a specified amount of time (usually about fifteen to thirty minutes). Younger children may be given a stack of picture books if they are not yet reading. Make sure the television and phone ringer are turned off. What an excellent way to model the love of reading, plus you can get some reading done yourself!

- ***Between the Lions-*** This television series is the winner of three Emmy Awards. It is available in many libraries and for purchase from PBS. This popular literacy series for preschool through third grade teaches basic language and reading concepts. Each segment has entertaining characters, songs, stories, animation, and live action.

- **Closed-caption television-** Studies indicate that using this feature on your television in reasonable doses can have a significant impact on your child's comprehension and vocabulary development. You can also play children's sing along videos for your child, which gives him the opportunity to demonstrate his word recognition skills while singing and dancing to his favorite songs.

- **Bookmarks**- Have your child use a bookmark if he is progressing to books with lots of lines per page since it is common for children to lose their place while reading. You can motivate your child by putting stickers on his bookmark for each book he reads.

- **Interactive learning games**- Computer games, such as The Learning Company's *Reader Rabbit* and Knowledge Adventure's *Jumpstart*, and electronic games, such as Vtech's *V. Smile*, LeapFrog's *Leapster* and *Leap Pad Learning System*, are magnificent ways to practice reading skills. These are especially helpful for kinesthetic learners. Some of the electronic games are portable, so your child can be learning while in the car, waiting for appointments, and on vacations.

- **Variations**- Keep in your home a wide variety of high-interest reading materials for your child, which may include: a *Guinness Book of World Records*, children's magazines, newspapers, question and answer books, comic books, joke books, poetry collections, and science books. Do not get into the habit of using only schoolbooks, as those can limit your child's reading expectations. The goal is to get your child to read for pleasure.

- **Books on cassettes and compact discs**- Children receive so much visual stimulation from television, computers, and video games that they are seriously lacking in listening skills. There are audio cassettes with picture books available in libraries for young children, who enjoy following along with the different narrators' voices. For older children, books are available on audio cassettes and compact discs. These are a great way to pass the time on long trips, and they are especially wonderful options for auditory learners.

- **Book-It**- Pizza Hut sponsors this reading incentive program. The parent chooses a reading goal, such as a minimum number of minutes, pages, or books per month. If your child meets his goal for the month, he receives a free personal pan pizza from Pizza Hut. Participating Pizza Hut restaurants reward the children with a medal at the end of the school year if all the monthly goals have been met. You can plan a trip to the restaurant with friends for a monthly pizza party to motivate your child even more.

- **Library reading programs**- Many public libraries offer reading incentive programs. Check your local library for additional information.

- **Taping sessions**- When a young child can read a book independently, record him reading on a cassette or video. Give this book on tape to a family member or friend. It is even fun to mail a copy to grandparents.

- **Book Adventure**- Sylvan sponsors my favorite reading resource, which is available at *www.bookadventure.com*. First, pick your child's reading level, and have your child choose five categories of interest. Next, print out a list of the books on your child's reading level that he would be interested in reading. Take the list to the library to find the books, or search your local library on-line to order the books.

  The best part is that your child can take a comprehension quiz on-line when he is finished reading the book. The program grades the quiz and rewards your child with points. Your child can go to the "prize center" on-line. Parents make up their own prizes, such as fifty points to stay up late one night, one hundred points for a trip to the movies, seventy-five points for a sleepover with a friend, thirty points for a trip to get ice cream, and one hundred fifty points to get one "free day" off from school. You choose what motivates your child. This free reading program is similar to the Accelerated Reader (AR) program that is used in many schools.

  If your child is consistently scoring high on the comprehension quizzes, you may be able to increase his reading level. If your child is repeatedly performing poorly, have your child read at a little lower level. The goal is to have your child reading material at his instructional level that is not too hard or too easy, but just right. Studies indicate the most efficient learning takes place when children stretch themselves a bit. If the material is too hard, your child may not be capable of processing it. If it is too easy, little growth may take place. Have fun using this awesome teaching tool!

- **Include high quality literature-** I strongly recommend having your child read high quality literature as soon as he can read independently. Many reading programs include their own books, which are often not very interesting. Instead, use superior quality books that are available from your local library.

  Have your child read as many children's classics as possible. Go on-line to *www.hbook.com/pdf/childrensclassics.pdf* for a list of children's classics with descriptions arranged by age group. Sometimes there are movies available that you can watch together as a family after your child has read the book. This will bring the book to life, and you can discuss how the movie was different from the book since movies often omit parts and change things for entertainment purposes.

  Newbery Medal and Caldecott Medal books are exceptional choices. The Newbery Medal was first offered in 1921 by Frederic Melcher and is donated annually to the most distinguished contribution in American children's literature. It was named after John Newbery, the famous eighteenth century publisher and seller of children's books.

  In addition, the Melcher family offered the first Caldecott Medal in 1938 to the artist of the most distinguished American picture book, and they continue to donate it annually. The award was named after Randolph Caldecott, the famous English illustrator of books for children. These award-winning books are extraordinary and can easily be incorporated into your existing curriculum. See the Appendix for a complete listing of these books.

- **Sight words**- These are words good readers instantly recognize without having to "figure them out." There are two reasons why sight words are an essential component of good reading. First, many of these words do not sound like their spellings might suggest, so "sounding them out" would be unproductive. Second, a good reader cannot afford the time to dwell on too many words, or he may lose the speed and fluency necessary for determining the author's message.

E.W. Dolch prepared this list of two hundred and twenty words, which makes up fifty to seventy-five percent of the words in reading material encountered by children. These words are generally known as Dolch Words, high-frequency words, or sight words. (Fry, Kress, and Fountoukidis, 2000, *The Reading Teacher's Book of Lists*: Jossey-Bass Publishing)

Dolch's List of Basic Sight Words

the	so	got	myself	pick
to	see	take	round	hurt
and	not	where	tell	pull
he	were	every	much	cut
a	get	pretty	keep	kind
I	them	jump	give	both
you	like	green	work	sit
it	one	four	first	which
of	this	away	try	fall
in	my	old	new	carry
was	would	by	must	small
said	me	their	start	under
his	will	here	black	read
that	yes	saw	white	why
she	big	call	ten	own
for	went	after	does	found
on	are	well	bring	wash
they	come	think	goes	slow
but	if	ran	write	hot
had	now	let	always	because
at	long	help	drink	far
him	no	make	once	live
with	came	going	soon	draw

up	ask	sleep	made	clean
all	very	brown	run	grow
look	an	yellow	gave	best
is	over	five	open	upon
her	yours	six	has	these
there	its	walk	find	sing
some	ride	two	only	together
out	into	or	us	please
as	just	before	three	thank
be	blue	eat	our	wish
have	red	again	better	many
go	from	play	hold	shall
we	good	who	buy	laugh
am	any	been	funny	what
then	about	may	warm	put
little	around	stop	ate	too
down	want	off	full	today
do	don't	never	those	fly
can	how	seven	done	say
could	know	eight	use	light
when	right	cold	fast	did

You enable your child to increase his reading efficiency when you teach him to read half or more of the words he encounters in a quick and automatic manner. Your teaching goal should be to have your child recognize these essential sight words within one second, preferably by the end of second grade.

Good evaluation procedures require these words be arranged in random order, not alphabetical order. I recommend breaking up the list into groups of ten words and focusing exclusively on just one group per week. Write the words on index cards two times each, and play "Memory" with them. Use these index cards also as flashcards to help your child to learn to read these words quickly. This approach will give you plenty of time to cover and review the entire list in one school year. In addition, have your child learn to spell these words correctly since they are also the most common words in writing. The first column alone in this list makes up about one-third of our written material.

🕮 **Word families-** Nearly five hundred primary words can be derived from this specific set of thirty-seven word families by adding letters in the beginning and at the end. (Marilyn Adams, 1990, *Beginning to Read: Thinking and Learning about Print*, Cambridge: MIT Press)

Word Families

ack	all	ain	ake	ale
ame	an	ank	ap	ash
at	ate	aw	ay	eat
ell	est	ice	ick	ide
ight	ill	in	ine	ing
ink	ip	ir	ock	oke
op	ore	or	uck	ug
ump	unk			

Take one or two word families per week, and write them in large print on a dry erase board. Have your child call out letters for you to write in the beginning and at the end. If it makes a word, your child copies the word on his paper. Try to see how many different words you can create together. Read aloud all of the words from his paper when you are finished. You can even have your child practice spelling these words.

Next, count the number of words on your child's paper, and try to beat that number the next time you play the "Word Family" game. Remember to turn simple lessons into games, and give your child goals to strive for to make learning easier and more enjoyable.

- **Work it out-** Children are always being told to "sound it out" when trying to read an unfamiliar word, but this does not always work for struggling readers. When your child comes to a word he cannot pronounce, try to find smaller chunks within the word that he may already know. Word families can really help with this. If your child still cannot determine the word, have him skip it, and finish reading the sentence. Help him use context clues from the sentence to figure out the word.

- **Use the five-finger method-** The best learning takes place when at least ninety-five percent of the words in a text can be read without difficulty. If your child struggles with more than five percent of the words, he cannot maintain fluency and comprehension. When starting a new book, your child can raise a finger each time he encounters a word he cannot read. If he has raised five fingers while reading a page or two (depending on how many words are on each page), the book may be too difficult.

  Harder reading material will not necessarily speed up your child's progress; it might actually hinder it. A good rule of thumb is to have your child start with a lower level, rather than too high, and continue to progress. You want to build up your child's confidence.

- **Be patient-** For children who are not yet reading independently, do not panic. Learning to read is developmental, just like riding a bike. If your child is not developmentally ready to ride a bike, you are not going to continue to put him on it day after day. You may wait a few weeks or months and try again. This same concept can be applied in reading.

  The most important thing you can do is read aloud to your child. He is learning many reading skills when you do this, and you will soon see the benefits. Besides reading aloud, practice the letter sounds and engage your child in mental exercises, such as puzzles and mazes. These activities will help your child's brain make important neurological connections, which set the foundation for reading.

- **Do not compare-** One of the most detrimental things parents can do while teaching reading is compare children's reading levels.

There is not any conclusive evidence early readers will excel faster and perform better in future school years when compared to late readers. I have seen children that could not read fluently until third grade, but they surpassed their classmates in reading skills within a year.

Let's go back to the bike-riding example. A child may not learn to ride for months or even years after his friends. But, that child may ride his bike faster and better than his friends when he finally masters that skill. Do not fall into the comparison trap. Learn to appreciate children's differences.

Book Reports

Book reports are excellent tools to improve comprehension and summarization skills. If your child completes a book report, let it count as his main writing assignment for the week.

There are many different genres of children's literature: fairy tales, folktales, myths, ballads, fables, nursery rhymes, science fiction, fantasies, historical fiction, realistic fiction, biography, informational, and poetry. Encourage your child to read in all of the genres for his book reports. This will expose him to a wide variety of literature.

It is a good idea for older children to complete a written report a few times each school year. Here are some guidelines you can use.

Written Book Report

I. Introduction
Include the title and author. Describe the setting and the main characters.

II. Body
Write a summary of the events in the story for a fiction book.
Summarize the written information for a nonfiction book.

III. Conclusion
For a fiction book, tell the events that resolve the conflict.
For a nonfiction book, summarize the main points in the body.

IV. Evaluation
Be specific about what was most enjoyable and what could have made it better. Tell whom you would recommend reading this book.

Your child does not always have to complete the traditional written report. Here are some creative alternatives for book reports.

- Write a letter to a main character in the book or the author of the book. You can even mail it to the author, and you may be surprised to see how many authors actually reply.
- Pretend your child is a radio broadcaster, and have him make an informative advertisement for the book. Record him on a cassette tape, and play it on your stereo's cassette player. This is fantastic for informational books.
- Chapter X- If your child wishes his book had never ended or that the ending was different, this may be for him. Write an additional chapter.
- Create a comic book of all the main events in the book. This is terrific for children who like to draw.
- Make a diorama. This is a timeless classic. A diorama is usually made inside a small box, such as a shoebox. The background is drawn, painted, or pasted inside the box. The diorama shows a favorite scene of a story. Nurture your child's creativity.
- Create a television commercial for the book. Tell the audience why the book should be purchased. Be persuasive and include props. Be careful not to give the ending away. Videotape your child, so he can watch himself on television. Let him be a star.
- Design a new book jacket. Your child can use the computer for graphics if he prefers. Include a summary of the book, and write a brief biography about the author for the back cover.
- Extra! Extra! Read all about it! Write an editorial review of the book that would be appropriate for a newspaper or magazine.
- Create a test or quiz about the book. Your child may write true and false, multiple choice, matching, and essay questions. Make sure to include an answer key. Let your child be the teacher, and you take the test. I hope you pass.

- Make a puppet of a main character, put on a puppet show, and write a character sketch that highlights several important characteristics or personality traits.

- Give a "Book-Talk" dressed as a main character in the book. Tell the audience specific reasons to read the book. Make it sound so good that everyone will want to read it. Do not forget the video camera.

- Make a timeline of the major events pertaining to the main character in the book. This is excellent for biographies.

- Create a puzzle by drawing on construction paper or poster board a favorite scene or the setting from the book. Cut the illustration into at least five puzzle pieces. Put the pieces into a plastic bag, and have someone put it together.

- Start your own monthly book club. Each month members in the book club can read a book from a predetermined genre or theme. Everyone can complete a project, and give an oral report or presentation to the group. This is great for practicing public speaking skills.

Encourage a love of reading.

You are your child's role model. If your child sees you reading for enjoyment, chances are he will learn to do the same. Use D.E.A.R. time in your home where everyone reads, including parents. Your goal is to instill a love of reading in your child that will last a lifetime.

We have a strong advantage over children who are sent to school. Those children are given a predetermined list of books to read. Our children have the opportunity to choose books that interest them. Have available a wide variety of high-interest reading material in your home, and let your child be your guide as long as he is reading at his instructional level.

Take your child to the bookstore for rewards and special occasions. Many bookstores offer substantial discounts to home educators. I am thankful for libraries, but there is something special about walking into a bookstore. There is a new adventure waiting to be explored, and your child has your full permission to go and find it. There is a sense of ownership when a child buys a book that connects him to the book even more. Let your child purchase a book, and observe his enthusiasm while he reads it.

Allow your child to enjoy evening reading. I tell my children they have a bedtime, but they can stay up later if they want. The catch is they must be in bed at a specified time, yet they can read any books to extend their bedtime up to thirty minutes. It is amazing how my oldest son will gladly read at night, even though he would never pick up a book if he was given the opportunity to watch television or play a video game. Reading can be relaxing and help children fall asleep easier at night. Why do you think bedtime stories are so popular?

Reading can be enjoyable for all. Do not get stressed about the small stuff, but thank God for the opportunity to watch your child learn to read. It is a big milestone in your child's life, and you are fortunate to be there to observe it all.

It took over an hour, but Deb finally explained what an adjective is.

CHAPTER 4

♥♥♥

WONDERFUL WRITING STRATEGIES

It is the supreme art of the teacher to awaken joy in creative expression and knowledge.

~Albert Einstein

Once the little ones begin to read, parents often need direction on writing. There are several essential components to writing effectively, which include grammar, handwriting, spelling, and writing skills.

GRAMMAR

Children absorb grammar from the people around them. Therefore, your child is more than likely using correct grammar before you ever try to teach it. Do not get consumed with teaching grammar rules and completing workbook exercises in the elementary years.

Do you remember doing *Mad Libs* as a kid? These are a fantastic way to practice the parts of speech. I leave a *Mad Libs* in my car's glove compartment, and I pull it out when we are on long road trips or when we have to wait in traffic. We like to read and laugh at my family's hilarious creations.

Schoolhouse Rock-Grammar Rocks video is excellent for teaching grammar rules to visual and auditory learners. I can still sing "Conjunction Junction" from watching Saturday morning cartoons as a child.

For upper elementary children, spend time searching for a language arts textbook that will not create burnout in your child. Pick and choose which skills are the most applicable for the school year. You can use one textbook for several years, and choose different skills to focus on each year. Keep in mind, publishing companies always provide more than what is needed. I prefer using grammar assignments only two days per week for the upper grades, so I have an ample amount of time to address writing.

A veteran homeschooling mother wisely stated, "You can briefly teach the key points of grammar in the elementary years and then get a good comprehensive grammar program in the middle school years to teach all the other skills. This method rules out all the repetition."

Instead of filling out workbook pages, your child can actually be writing and learning the mechanics of writing at the same time. Your writing goal is to make your child a proficient writer, not to complete textbooks.

HANDWRITING

There are many terrific handwriting programs, but some parents do not realize they also need to purchase paper in different sizes for writing assignments in the primary grades. Kindergarten typically starts off with a 1" spacing. Next, children graduate to ⅝" and then to ½" spacing. Do not move to the smaller lines until your child has neat, legible handwriting on the larger lines.

The best quality penmanship paper I have found for the primary years is available at *www.millerpadsandpaper.com.* I do not recommend notebook paper until the fourth grade. Use wide-ruled paper, not college-ruled.

Keep a reference sheet with all the letters of the alphabet written correctly for your young child to refer to when completing writing assignments. I use a laminated placemat with the alphabet on it that has lasted for years. Jumbo pencils are also available for young writers. These pencils fit perfectly in little hands to reduce writer's cramp.

Children must build upper body, arm, hand, and finger strength to improve fine-motor skills. If your child is struggling with handwriting, have him do the following activities to develop strength, precision, and hand-eye coordination.

- Play with clay, play dough, or Floam.

- Complete children's sewing activities, such as lacing shapes.

- Use playground equipment, such as monkey bars and climbing apparatuses.
- Participate in extra-curricular activities, such as swimming, gymnastics, and karate.
- Complete dot-to-dots, mazes, and puzzles.
- Dry silverware with a towel.
- Make sandwiches by spreading ingredients on bread, such as peanut butter and jelly.
- Play games that involve shuffling and passing out cards, rolling dice while cupped in his hands, and handling small game pieces.
- Thread Fruit Loops on a string or use lacing bead activities.
- Spear grapes and other small fruit pieces with a toothpick.
- Play with small toys, such as Legos, Tinkertoys, Lincoln Logs, action figures, and blocks.
- Use drawing books and stencils to create illustrations.
- Learn to tie shoes and button clothes.
- Complete creative art projects that involve the following: crayons, markers, colored pencils, finger paints, and scissors.
- Pull small weeds.
- Play musical instruments.
- Sort collections of loose coins into stacks of pennies, nickels, dimes, and quarters.
- Play with math manipulatives, such as pattern blocks, stacking pegs, and Geoboards.
- Play with an Etch-a-Sketch or a Magna Doodle.

Handwriting Without Tears is an outstanding program to use with children who are having a difficult time with fine motor skills because it uses multi-sensory techniques for letter formation. Activities with wood pieces, letter cards, roll-a-dough letters, the stamp and see screen, and the slate chalkboard use all of the senses to teach directionality, positioning, and sequencing skills. Double lines are unique to this curriculum, which end the problem of line confusion

What do you do to practice handwriting with children who can already write letters correctly? The *Draw Write Now* series by Marie Hablitzel and Kim Stitzer is the answer. A former second-grade teacher designed this program to add creativity to the daily mundane task of handwriting. First, children write several sentences on a subject that relates to a science or social studies theme. The next day, they develop their fine motor skills by drawing shapes and creating illustrations that correspond to their sentences. Use writing paper with this program that has the top portion blank for illustrations and the bottom portion with lines for sentences.

This is a unique approach to handwriting that children like, even those who do not particularly enjoy handwriting. I am impressed that they are also learning to write complete sentences with capital letters and correct punctuation. In addition, the children are learning science and social studies facts. You can't go wrong here!

Once your child is legibly writing his letters and words correctly in complete sentences, you can stop teaching handwriting as a separate subject. You can evaluate his handwriting in his writing assignments instead.

SPELLING

The first major decision you must make when teaching spelling is choosing the words you would like your child to learn. I prefer not to use spelling textbooks. Observe carefully which skills most spelling books address. The majority of textbooks teach reading skills, such as filling in the blanks in sentences, and grammar skills, such as labeling words with the correct parts of speech. These are great skills to learn, but your child should already be learning these skills during your reading and grammar instructional time. Your goal should be to teach your child how to spell words correctly during your spelling instructional time.

Most curriculums also teach spelling rules. Young children seldom apply rules in spelling. Research has repeatedly shown less than ten spelling rules are actually worth learning in the English language. How does a child correctly spell a word in his writing? The word looks and feels right, not from applying spelling rules.

Reading a lot is the key to growing vocabulary and spelling skills. The most effective way of choosing vocabulary and spelling words is to select words from your child's reading, science, and social studies books.

For early readers, use words from the basic sight words list (see p. 34-35). These are not only the most common words in reading but in writing as well. I would much rather teach my child the most common words in writing before a chosen list of words from a textbook. You can also make your own lists from the word families (see p. 36).

My college professor presented study after study on the effectiveness of writing out spelling words multiple times. Surprisingly, every bit of research proved this is an ineffective way of teaching spelling. What? I had to write my spelling words five times each all the time as a child. I was shocked to learn all of my hard work had no educational benefits!

Here are some sensational ideas on how to teach spelling with a creative approach that lead to true learning. Hold on to your seats! You probably never knew spelling could be so much fun.

- Rainbow write with markers, colored pencils, or crayons. Use different colors for every other letter. You can use variations, such as red and green for Christmas, blue and red for patriotic themes, and orange and brown for Thanksgiving. You can also use one color for vowels and a different color for consonants.

- Use shaving cream on a table to write the words. Have your child smooth it out with his hands for a writing surface and use his finger as his writing tool.

- Put Jell-O powder or cake mix evenly onto paper plates, and have your child lick his finger as he spells the words.

- Paint the words with watercolors or finger paints.

- Have your child act, dance, or do jumping jacks for the letters in the words. This is my favorite activity for those energetic days.

- Write the words on black construction paper with a white piece of chalk, a white crayon, or gel pens.

- Use flashlights to spell the words on a wall in a dark room.
- Type the words.
- Write the words on a partner's back with a finger while the partner tries to guess them.
- Use alphabet stickers to spell the words.
- Write the words with glue. Put beans, macaroni, or other small items on the glue.
- Play hangman with the words.
- Write a story with the spelling words.
- Play memory with the words on index cards.
- Use pipe cleaners to form the letters in the words.
- Write the words outside with sidewalk chalk.
- Use alphabet magnets to make the words on the refrigerator.
- Find the words or letters in newspapers and magazines, and make a collage.
- Use small chalkboards or dry-erase boards to write the words on.
- Clap or snap each letter of the words with rhythm.
- Use pretzel sticks, licorice string, M&Ms, Cheerios, raisins, or beans to form the letters in the words.
- Write the words on large grid graph paper. This is great for words with double letters.
- Use popsicle sticks or straws to form the letters in the words.
- Play Scrabble using only spelling words.

- Write the words with a popsicle stick in a sandbox or a shallow pan filled with uncooked rice.
- Have a spelling bee for an end-of-the-year review.
- Make a word search using large grid graph paper. Write the spelling words in the squares. Encourage your child to make his word search as difficult as possible. Fill in the leftover spaces with the alphabet. Have a parent, sibling, or friend find the words. This is a favorite of children of all ages.

Aren't you excited? Some of these spelling ideas can be also used for fine-motor skills in handwriting. If you still prefer using a spelling book, you can substitute some of the exercises in the textbook with these hands-on activities to spice things up a bit.

I recommend giving your child an oral pretest in the beginning of the week. If your child has ten words for spelling but spells half of them correctly on an oral pretest, he needs to only practice five words that week. There is no need to continue practicing words your child can already spell. This is an efficient way to manage your teaching time. Now, let's use those correctly spelled words in writing.

WRITING SKILLS
Kindergarten-Second Grade

For the primary grades, your main goal is to have your child write a complete sentence, which consists of a complete thought with a noun and a verb and includes correct capitalization and punctuation. This may sound very basic, but writing is developmental like reading. Be aware it may take some time for your child to master this concept.

One way to help your child learn writing skills is to provide lots of opportunities for modeling by writing out sentences and stories while your child narrates them. After narration, have your child read the sentences and add illustrations. This is also an excellent way to create books for beginning readers. Your child will love to read them again and again.

This is the foundation for kindergarten through second grade:

- ✓ In kindergarten, have your child write daily in his journal. Give him a story starter, such as "My best friend is __________." Initially, have him just complete the sentence. You will need to help guide him with spelling. Gradually progress to having your child copy and complete the entire sentence. Have your child illustrate his writing. Children like to draw and color, which improves their fine motor skills.

- ✓ In first grade, begin with story starters and slowly progress to topics, such as "Write about what you did this weekend." Your child will write one or more sentences.

- ✓ By second grade, your child will correctly write several sentences about a topic. This is setting the stage for writing paragraphs. If you have a difficult time thinking of story starters and topics, just search the Internet with the keywords "writing prompts" for an endless supply of free ideas.

I strongly encourage you to choose the most important concepts to mark incorrectly on your child's papers. It is discouraging for a child to have his paper covered with corrections after he worked so hard on his masterpiece. Always praise your child, and only mark a few things wrong at a time. Most importantly, you want your child to be able to confidently express himself on paper. Put stickers on his final copy, and make him feel like he accomplished something outstanding!

Third Grade

I have categorized these goals by grade levels, so you can see what your child would be learning in a typical school setting. Do not progress to this level until your child is writing multiple sentences correctly on a specific topic.

Around third grade, students are introduced to the writing process, which is located on the following page. These are the stages your child works through while writing, which need to be consistently reinforced throughout the upper elementary grades. Address one to two stages of the writing process per day. On day one, brainstorm ideas with your child. On day two, have your child write his sloppy copy. Children can catch many of their own mistakes if you give them some time between writing lessons and they read it aloud. On day three, make a neat sheet. On day four, proofread the neat sheet, and make the final copy. Always have your child share his final copy.

The Writing Process

(1) Pre-writing (brainstorming)
(2) Rough draft (sloppy copy)
(3) Revising (neat sheet)
(4) Editing (proofreading)
(5) Publishing (final copy)

The 3.5 paragraph is one of the main writing concepts of third grade. The formula for a 3.5 paragraph is three ideas and five sentences.

3.5 Paragraph

(1) Introductory topic sentence with three ideas
(2) Detail sentence about idea #1
(3) Detail sentence about idea #2
(4) Detail sentence about idea #3
(5) Concluding sentence

The following is an example of a third-grader's 3.5 paragraph:

In the future, I want to become a race car driver, a sports announcer, or an astronaut. I like fast cars, so I want to race in the Indy 500. Also, I became interested in being a sports announcer when I visited my uncle who works for NBC-TV. It really would be exciting to work at a space station and travel to Mars. If any of these dreams come true, I will be happy!

A wonderful visual aid you can use to teach the 3.5 paragraph is a "Paragraph Train." Have your child make an engine, three cars, and a caboose out of construction paper. Have him label the following parts: the engine is the topic sentence; the three cars are the detail sentences;

and the caboose is the concluding sentence. When the train is complete, your child knows he is finished writing his paragraph.

You may also use a hamburger as a visual aid. Have your child make a hamburger with construction paper. Have him label the following parts: the top bun is the topic sentence; the tomato, lettuce, and hamburger patty are the detail sentences; and the bottom bun is the concluding sentence. These visual aids make writing fun.

For 3.5 paragraph writing prompts, use information from your child's science and social studies lessons. For instance, have your child write three facts describing a country he is studying in social studies or an animal he is learning about in science.

Narrative writing, sometimes known as creative story writing, is also encouraged in third grade. Narrative writing includes the beginning, middle, and end.

Narrative Writing

Beginning- Introduce the characters and setting.
Middle- Create the problem or action.
End- Explain the conclusion or a solution to the story.

Your child can use *Story Starters Write-Abouts* by McDonald Publishing Company to choose a character, setting, and plot to create a story. This flipbook provides a unique way of actively involving your child in selecting writing prompts. I also like to use *Kid Talk Conversation Cards* by U.S. Games Systems because they provide children with background knowledge by setting the stage for the writing prompts. Additional ideas for narrative writing prompts can be found on the Internet.

Encourage your child not to use the words "The End." Use a detailed closing sentence instead. You can have your child use graphic organizers (see p. 27) to help with brainstorming. There are multiple websites on the Internet where you can print free story maps. Search the keywords "graphic organizer."

You can alternate a 3.5 paragraph one week with narrative writing the next week. For narrative writing, I strongly suggest you purchase "bare books" at *www.barebooks.com.* These inexpensive, hard-cover books have blank pages your child can write his final copy on, and he can turn his story into a real book to share with others. You can print graphics for the cover, and use clear contact paper to protect it. Even in middle school, my oldest son still makes a few of these each year for fun.

These are the basic writing skills for this grade level and beyond.

Writing Skills

Complete sentences
Capitalization
Punctuation
Indention of paragraphs
Transition words
Descriptive language
Usage of a dictionary for correct spelling
Usage of a thesaurus for synonyms

Fourth Grade

Fourth grade writing consists mostly of expository (essay) writing and narrative (story) writing. Use writing prompts from your reading, science, and social studies units for the expository writings. Use narrative writing prompts from the Internet. Remember to work through the writing process, and cover all of the writing skills continuously.

Make reference sheets with transition words, capitalization rules, and punctuation rules, and keep them in your child's writing folder. When you begin your writing lesson, spread these reference sheets on the table since your child does not have visual aids to guide him like those found in a classroom setting. Encourage your child to use a thesaurus to find descriptive words and a dictionary to check his spelling.

Once the 3.5 paragraph is mastered, your child will progress to the next level, which is expository writing. He is still using three ideas, but now he is writing a paragraph about each idea instead of a sentence. Thus, there will be five paragraphs instead of five sentences.

The easiest way I have found to help children organize their expository writing is by using the traditional outline format during the pre-writing stage. Your child can use colored pencils to underline topic sentences in one color and detail sentences in another color on his outline and rough draft. This will help him identify the topics and details for each.

You will need to complete the first few outlines and essays with your child. Patiently talk your child through each step, and help your child add plenty of details to his sentences. After your child understands the concept, have him complete the outline with your guidance, but let him independently write his rough draft using his outline. The last step will be to have your child make up his own outline without instruction, and write the essay independently. Writing an essay may take awhile to master so be patient. This skill is a major writing component and will continue to be used throughout college.

Expository Writing

I. Introductory paragraph with three topics

II. Topic #1
a. Detail about topic #1
b. Detail about topic #1
c. Detail about topic #1

III. Topic #2
a. Detail about topic#2
b. Detail about topic#2
c. Detail about topic#2

IV. Topic #3
a. Detail about topic #3
b. Detail about topic #3
c. Detail about topic #3

V. Concluding paragraph

Fifth and Sixth Grade

For fifth and sixth grade, continue narrative writing and expository writing with the outline format. Students performing at these grade levels are ready to begin writing persuasive essays.

Persuasive Essay

Introduction- State your opinion.
Body- Write three paragraphs that support your opinion. Use facts and examples. Justify your strongest or most important reason last.
Conclusion- Restate your opinion. Ask your reader to take action.

A common mistake at this writing level is children often forget to put a comma before conjunctions when combining two independent sentences. Another frequent error is the constant use of "and then." Have your child use transition words instead, such as: furthermore, therefore, meanwhile, in addition, although, on the other hand, however, next, for instance, for example, first, second, third, last, finally, overall, in conclusion, and in summary.

Put a writing checklist in your child's writing folder to help him edit his own work. You can make copies of this checklist, or make up your own. Your goal at this stage is to get your child writing independently without constant reminders.

Writing Checklist

___I have a creative title.
___I read my writing assignment aloud to check meaning.
___I indented all of my paragraphs.
___I began my sentences with a capital letter.
___I put the correct punctuation marks at the end of my sentences.
___I put commas in the correct places, including before conjunctions when needed.
___I used several transition words.
___I used at least ten descriptive words.
___I checked my spelling.

Have your child type his final copy. This is great practice for typing skills. You can print all of his writing assignments at the end of the school year, and bind them into a book at a copy center. Publishing their writing makes children feel important, and this is a vital part for motivation.

Integrate writing assignments into other subjects you are teaching to make them more interesting. There are many other writing assignments you can address, such as letter writing, poetry, book reports, and writing step-by-step directions. Writing takes a lot of practice to master. The key is to get your child not to dislike writing assignments but to motivate and inspire him through this process. I hope you now realize writing does not have to be a difficult process or taken from an expensive program. Just concentrate on a few goals each year, and your child will be on his way to success. Write on!

CHAPTER 5

♥♥♥

MAGNIFICENT MATH TECHNIQUES

The art of teaching is the art of assisting discovery.

~Pablo Casals

Mathematics is everywhere and every day is filled with opportunities to help children experience it. You probably remember studying arithmetic (addition, subtraction, multiplication, and division) when you were in elementary school. Children are now learning about the broad ideas associated with math, which include problem solving, communicating mathematically, and demonstrating reasoning ability.

A problem solver is someone who questions, investigates, and explores solutions to problems. He understands that there may be different ways to arrive at an answer and applies math to everyday situations. You can encourage your child to be a good problem solver by involving him in decision-making processes using math.

To communicate mathematically means to use words, numbers, or symbols to explain mathematical situations. You can help your child learn to communicate mathematically by asking him to explain a math problem or answer, write about the process he used, or draw a picture of how he arrived at an answer to a problem.

Reasoning ability means thinking logically while being able to see similarities and differences between things. Have your child explain his answers to math problems. As you listen, you will hear your child sharing his reasoning.

There are three fundamental steps to making your math teaching time the most effective. Make sure your instructional time includes a superior math program as your foundation, math games, and manipulatives (various objects used to understand abstractions).

Math Programs

As home educators, we are fortunate to have many terrific math programs to choose from. A Beka's math program is my top choice. These inexpensive, colorful workbooks use a spiral review method that builds on concepts previously learned. If your child is not developmentally ready to learn a skill, A Beka provides constant repetition to give him a chance to grasp the skill at a later time. I add more manipulatives to enhance its hands-on activities.

I also recommend *Math-U-See* because it uses a hands-on approach to learning mathematical skills. This program simultaneously emphasizes computation skills and conceptual understanding. It is especially effective for kinesthetic learners. If your child enjoys working primarily with manipulatives versus a paper and pencil approach, this program may work well for him.

If you become frustrated with teaching math to your upper elementary child, *Switched-On Schoolhouse* by Alpha Omega Publications offers a comprehensive math curriculum designed to exceed state standards. It is a self-directed program that is completed on a computer. The program grades the work, and you can print reports to check your child's progress.

Regardless of which math program you have chosen for your child, I am going to give you some additional teaching ideas you can incorporate into any math curriculum.

Math Manipulatives

One mistake parents often make is purchasing math textbooks but forgetting the hands-on part of teaching mathematics. In addition to the math program your child uses, add many hands-on activities and games. These will help your child understand important math concepts and allow him to progress from concrete manipulation to abstract thinking.

For the primary years, there are many manipulatives available to help create a strong foundation in math. It is usually more economical to buy these manipulatives in sets. However, you do not need to purchase all of these manipulatives since it can be a large investment. You can go on the Internet to the On-line National Library of Virtual Manipulatives. It takes the use of manipulatives to a whole new level. Here are the manipulatives I recommend using:

- **Colored plastic links-** Use for counting, addition, subtraction, sorting, measurement, patterns, and sequences.
- **Cuisenaire rods-** Use for addition, subtraction, multiplication, division, area, bar graphs, and measurement. Make sure to purchase the track for the rods, too.
- **Base Ten Blocks-** Use for number operations, place value, area, volume, and fractions.
- **Tangrams-** Use for shape recognition, size comparison, spatial reasoning, and geometry.
- **Pattern Blocks-** Use for measurement, shape recognition, fractional relationships, spatial reasoning, and geometry.
- **Geoboards-** Use for spatial relationships, angles, fractions, area, perimeter, symmetry, and coordinates.
- **Fraction circles-** Use for fractional relationships. There are even magnetic circles and pizza fractions available.
- **Fraction equivalency cubes-** Use for fractional relationships.
- **Unifix cubes-** Use for patterns, fractions, probability, addition, subtraction, multiplication, division, place value, measurement, and graphing.
- **Teaching clock-** Use for time-telling skills for analog clocks.
- **Number line-** Use for addition and subtraction.

- **Counting bears-** Use for addition, subtraction, multiplication, division, patterns, and probability.

- **3-D shapes-** Use these to search for relationships among the shapes, discover the connection between surface area and volume, and find out how three-dimensional shapes are related to their two-dimensional shapes.

- **Color counters-** Use for addition, subtraction, multiplication, division, and probability.

- **Hundreds number board-** Use for a wide variety of number explorations, including patterns and skip counting.

- **Primary rocker balance and scale-** Use for measurement of weight.

- **Spinners-** Use for probability.

Here are some manipulatives you may already have in your home:

- **Beans, raisins, buttons, Legos, Cheerios, Skittles, and M&M's**- Use for counting, patterns, addition, subtraction, multiplication, and division.

- **Popsicles sticks and straws**- Use for place-value and tally marks.

- **Dominoes-** Use for addition.

- **Calculator-** Use for meaningful problem solving activities and computation skills.

- **Thermometer-** Use for measurement of Fahrenheit and Celsius temperatures.

- **Real or play money-** Use for currency identification and values, equivalences, counting, and making change.

- **Ruler-** Use for linear measurement.

- **Dice-** Use for addition, subtraction, multiplication, and division.

If you are exclusively using a math workbook, include manipulatives every day in the early grades. For older children, use the manipulatives whenever your child is beginning a new concept or struggling with a skill.

Math Games

My thesis in graduate school was on the effectiveness of mathematical games. You would not believe how much faster children memorize facts when there is a game involved! Your child will be actively engaged in the learning process, which is much more effective than standard drills. Play a math game every other day in the primary grades and once a week in the upper elementary grades. Just say the words, "Let's play a game," and watch your child run to you!

Numerous studies have shown great improvements in math test scores in children who play chess, which is considered a required curriculum in nearly thirty countries. Chess can be used effectively as a tool to teach problem solving and abstract reasoning. Learning how to solve a problem is more important than learning the solution to any particular problem. Chess requires a mental workout by thinking ahead, planning, being systematic, and determining the outcomes of certain moves. Chess moves cannot be memorized. Weaknesses in math often originate from an over emphasis on memory skills instead of thinking skills.

Here are some other math games I recommend: Math Board Games (addition, subtraction, multiplication, and division) by Learning Resources, Addition/Subtraction and Multiplication Math War by School Zone, Money and Time Bingo by Trend Enterprises, and Math Wrap-Ups by Learning Wrap-Ups. Similar games with the same educational concepts are manufactured by different companies.

Some of the best games are created by parents and teachers. The following are some examples:

- **Dominoes with a twist-** This game helps children learn addition facts. Players take turns picking dominoes that are turned face down and adding up the dots. This is perfect for young children because they can count the dots on both sides of the dominoes and add them together. Have your child keep score with tally marks. Children get very little practice with tally marks in most textbooks. The person with the most points wins.

- **What's missing?-** This game uses small objects to practice subtraction facts. For instance, put nine beans on the table. Have your child count the objects. Ask your child to turn around. Hide five of the beans underneath a cup. Have your child turn back around and count the number of beans left on the table. Ask your child to guess "what's missing." Have him check his answer by looking underneath the cup to see the five beans. Continue using different subtraction facts.

- **Dice games-** There are many great math games with dice. You can play an addition game by rolling two dice and adding up the total. The first player to one hundred wins. You can later add a third die to practice adding three numbers. You can play a multiplication game by rolling two dice, multiplying them to get your product, and adding up the total. Remember to have your child keep score with tally marks.

  Circles and Stars is the best game I have used with children who are beginning to learn multiplication. Roll one die and make that many circles on your paper. Roll another die and make that many stars on the inside of each circle. Write out the multiplication sentence to go with that problem. Have your child count the stars in each circle for the total. For example, two circles with three stars in each circle equals six stars. (2 x 3 = 6) Take turns rolling the dice and illustrating the number sentences. Have your child add all the products (total amount of stars) each person has with a calculator to see who wins. If your child takes a long time drawing stars, you can use small star stickers or substitute Xs for stars, and rename the game "Xs and Os."

- **Mad minutes-** Make several copies of a math drill sheet. Give your child the same sheet every day for a week before you start your daily math lesson. Time him for one minute to see how many math facts he can answer correctly. Have him try to beat his record the next day. You can teach your child to answer the facts he knows first and then go back to the problems that take extra time. If he can answer at least ninety percent correctly within one minute by the end of the week, he can receive a reward. These are great for learning and reviewing the basic facts (addition, subtraction, multiplication, and division) in any grade level, and they only take one minute!

- ***Family Math***- Additional math games can be found in this popular book that is published by Equal Publications. This resource provides an interactive approach to understanding math concepts. The games listed in the book are easy-to-follow, engaging, and challenging.

Math Resources

- **Math Shark-** This is the best resource I have found for reviewing math skills. The Math Shark is a small, hand-held calculator. It has timed, self-directed games that drill seven math skills (addition, subtraction, multiplication, division, fractions, decimals, and percents) from the basic facts to pre-algebra level. It gives nonstop feedback with lights and sounds. You can use it on those days you may not get to math or if you have to do math on the go. It is also excellent for quick reviews of math facts in the summer, and it sure beats flashcards!

- **Math books**- Did you know you can use literature in math? Here are some examples of books that help explain elementary math concepts, which may be available at your local library:

    - *Each Orange Had 8 Slices* by Paul Giganti, Jr.- counting
    - *The M&M's Counting Book* by Barbara McGrath- counting
    - *Sea Squares* by Joy Hulme- multiplication
    - *The Doorbell Rang* by Pat Hutchins- division
    - *How Much is a Million?* by David Schwartz- large numbers
    - *If You Made a Million* by David Schwartz- money

- **Math video-** The *Schoolhouse Rock-Multiplication Rocks* video is ideal for visual and auditory learners.

- **Math songs-** There are addition, multiplication, and skip counting songs available on CDs and cassettes. These are fantastic for auditory learners.

- **Computer games-** The Learning Company's *Math Rabbit* and Knowledge Adventure's *Math Blaster* and *Jumpstart* are terrific games for practicing math skills, especially for kinesthetic learners.

Math Strategies

- **Basic facts-** Memorization of the basic facts (addition, subtraction, multiplication, and division) is imperative for excelling in elementary math. These facts set the foundation for other mathematical concepts. Your child should be able to give a correct answer in less than three seconds for complete mastery. Considerable drill is required for children to give quick responses. Use flash cards, games, songs, Math Wrap-Ups, and the Math Shark to help your child learn basic facts. When your child does not know an answer, have him use manipulatives.

- **Graph paper-** I encourage you to use graph paper while teaching math. Have your child write vertically two and three digit addition, subtraction, and multiplication problems. This helps eliminate regrouping mistakes. Using graph paper is also the best way to teach long division. Start with larger grid paper, and switch to smaller grids as your child works more independently.

- **Money management-** One of the best strategies I have used to teach my oldest son about money was giving him an allowance. I began by giving him one dollar per week in kindergarten. This dollar came with responsibility.

  I assign certain chores, such as cleaning his room, feeding the dog, and watering the plants. Each year he receives an extra dollar per week, along with one extra chore. I do not pay him for simply doing the chore but for completing it to my expectations. If he forgets to do a chore and I have to remind him, a deduction is made. You can adapt this procedure to meet your family's needs.

The benefits from this strategy are three-fold. First, my son learns each family member works together and shares responsibility in a home. Second, he learns life skills. Third, he learns to manage his money wisely.

My son has a My Learning ATM bank from Crown Financial Ministries that automatically divides up his money into giving, savings, and spending. He makes deposits and withdrawals with his ATM card. What a wonderful tool that teaches children how to be good stewards with their money at an early age!

My son has my permission to use his "spending money" on candy, a toy, a movie, or any other extras he wants. He pays for these things independently by giving the cashier his money and counting his change. This method eliminates him asking me for money, and it is amazing how conservative he is with his own money. He looks for coupons and waits for items to go on sale. He counts his money repeatedly. He uses problem solving skills and mental math to figure out how much more money he needs to save and how many weeks it will take him to achieve his goal. This strategy is as real-life as they come.

❖ **Long division tip**- I have to share with you an easy way to remember the long division process since long division seems to stump so many children. I have tutored children using this method with graph paper, and the results have been outstanding.

Long Division Helpful Hint

(1) Divide (Daddy)
(2) Multiply (Mother)
(3) Subtract (Sister)
(4) Bring down (Brother)

Have your child write the steps at the top of his paper before he starts his division problems. He can refer to the steps if he forgets what to do next while completing a problem. This will keep your child from constantly asking you for the next step when he gets stuck.

Explore math in everyday life, such as: counting cars when they pass you while driving, measuring ingredients when baking a cake, using coupons when grocery shopping, and telling the time during daily activities. When children realize math is all around them, they begin to relax and see its meaning in their lives. Have fun making math meaningful!

CHAPTER 6

♥♥

SOCIAL STUDIES & SCIENCE-
A FAMILY AFFAIR

What I hear, I may grasp.
What I see, I may remember.
What I do, I understand.

~ *Chinese Proverb*

Social studies and science should be the most exhilarating subjects to teach, yet many parents dislike teaching these subjects. This is primarily due to the majority of home educators exclusively using textbooks to teach these subjects, which drain all the excitement out.

When I taught elementary science and social studies in public school, I had no choice but to use the textbooks appointed by the school district. It was difficult keeping my students' interest using textbooks as the primary teaching tool. Therefore, I included many hands-on activities to enliven these subjects.

You have a choice as a homeschooling parent. Textbooks were created for classroom settings. Initially, excluding textbooks may be difficult because this is how most of us learned these subjects. As a former teacher, I was also conditioned in this way of teaching. It took me a few years to fully transition, but I am happily there. I have some great ideas to help you join me!

Get your feet wet.

If you feel like you cannot release your fingers from your textbook and would like to test the waters first, you can gradually incorporate science experiments, field trips, library books, and videos into chapters you are currently teaching. Teach from the textbook a couple of days then switch to other activities for the rest of the week. The basic premise is to use your textbook as a guide, not as your main teaching tool.

Dive in!

If you're ready to jump right in, come along with me. I planned my science lessons one year by asking my oldest son what he would be interested in learning. From *www.kidsdiscoverteachers.com*, I ordered magazines to correlate with his areas of interest and other concepts I wanted him to learn for the school year. You can browse through numerous titles for social studies and science on this website. There are teacher's guides available, too. I prefer *Kids Discover* magazines to textbooks because the illustrations are beautiful, and the concepts are taught in such an interesting manner that I even enjoy reading them.

One or two days a week would be devoted to the magazine. The other days I got books and videos from the library, went on field trips, and researched on-line for experiments and hands-on activities. We made learning fun! My children enjoy science and social studies so much that I save it for last. This way they can take their time learning and discovering without feeling rushed.

Unit studies in science and social studies are typically easier for parents who homeschool multiple children since you can learn science and social studies together as a family. If you like the unit studies approach but are afraid to venture out on your own, there are many publishing companies who sell unit study programs. These may work well for you.

Flip-flop subjects.

You can alternate science and social studies every other year. This enables you to completely focus on one particular subject area. For example, I used to plan a thirty minute block of time for social studies on Mondays and Tuesdays and a sixty minute block of time for science on

Wednesdays. Now, I use those three blocks of time for science one school year and social studies the following year. Therefore, I still devote the same amount of time (in my case, two hours per week) to each particular subject within a two-year period of time. This is not as confusing for the child, and there is less preparation for the parent.

Current Events

Regardless of whether I am teaching science or social studies for the year, I always teach current events. For the early grades, I use Scholastic's *Weekly Reader*. For the upper elementary grades, I prefer *News Current* from God's World News. These are both excellent resources that are mailed to your home each week. They are very economical and educational. I also use them for reading comprehension and vocabulary skills.

Science Experiments

Janice VanCleave's *Play and Find Out Science* series has simple experiments for children. Each experiment includes a list of easy-to-find materials, illustrations, and step-by-step instructions.

Robert Krampf's experiment of the week is available on the Internet. He provides fun and easy experiments using everyday household materials. The experiments are targeted for a wide range of students. Send a blank email to *krampf-subscribe@topica.com* to receive free weekly experiments.

If you have a hard time gathering the materials for experiments, you can purchase experiments that have the materials already included for you. My favorite pre-packaged science kits can be ordered from *www.holycowscience.com*. These kits are designed to teach important scientific principles while having fun. Each kit is formatted using the scientific method of inquiry and includes clearly written instructions and all of the required materials. This company also sells kits for science fair projects.

It is good for both parents to be included in homeschooling as much as possible. My husband enjoys doing science experiments with our children, so I leave that part of schooling to him. When you are conducting experiments at home, discuss the scientific method. Older children can write out the process.

Scientific Method

Purpose- What are you trying to find out?
Hypothesis- Make an educated guess of the predicted outcome.
Procedures- List all the materials used and step-by-step details of your plan during the experiment.
Data- Record your observations during the experiment.
Conclusion- Decide what your data tells you about your hypothesis. Was your hypothesis correct?

Videos

PBS has excellent videos available for social studies. One example is *Freedom: A History of U.S.*, which is an outstanding video series for teaching U.S. history to upper elementary children. Joy Hakim's books form the basis for this series chronicling America's commitment to liberty and the true meaning of freedom. I particularly enjoy listening to the character voices that belong to celebrities.

Children enjoy watching PBS's *Liberty Kids* because it features animated portrayals of historical figures. Students become reporters and discover the real heroes and events that gave birth to our nation.

My favorite video series is published by Nest Family Entertainment, which has biographies of famous people from a Christian perspective. The *Nest Family* videos come with booklets, so you can reproduce worksheets from them to correspond with the videos.

I like the *Eyewitness* science and social studies videos because they are very intriguing. These videos capture the audience's full attention while simultaneously filling them with educational facts.

Scholastic's *Magic School Bus* is the most entertaining science videos I have seen yet. I enjoy reading aloud the books to my children before we watch the videos.

There are some television channels that are known for their quality programs. Check out PBS, the Discovery Channel, and the History Channel on-line to preview program listings, so you can record and view the programs at your convenience. Their websites also offer educational games and teaching ideas.

Listening Skills

States and Capitals Songs and *Geography Songs* by Larry and Kathy Troxel teach the names of states, capitals, continents, oceans, planets, and two hundred twenty-five countries. *Wee Sing America* by Pamela Beall and Susan Nipp includes classic songs from America's past. These are extremely effective with auditory learners.

For older homeschooled children, there are few opportunities for practicing note-taking skills. One way to meet this need is by having your child write "five fascinating facts" he learned while watching science and social studies videos. This is truly a skill that must not be overlooked in preparation for high school and college classes.

Books and Magazines

Scholastic's *Magic School Bus* series features an eccentric school-teacher who takes her class on amazing educational field trips with the help of a magical school bus. These cute and educational books are enjoyed by children of all ages.

Mary Pope Osborne's *Magic Tree House* series includes adventurous books that have high-interest science and social studies themes. My oldest son literally could not put them down.

Usborne Publishing has a variety of spectacular choices for science and history. These books are very informative and wonderful to use for unit studies.

The *Dear America* series by Scholastic Publishing is very popular with realistic readings that make a time period jump to life. Do not assume the series is for girls only. This series is one of my favorites to read aloud to all children.

Harper & Brothers' *Little House* series is also a phenomenal series to read aloud. It is based on memories of Laura Ingalls Wilder's childhood in the Midwest region of the United States during the late nineteenth century.

Children Like Me by DK Publishing gives a remarkable insight into the lives of children all around the world. It conveys to the reader the unique diversity of the world's children while exploring the common bonds they share.

You can also add a different dimension to learning science and social studies by ordering monthly subscriptions to children's magazines. I recommend *Ranger Rick* for young children. *National Geographic Kids* and *Kids Discover* are great for older children. Your child will enjoy receiving his own mail each month.

Words of Caution

Be sure to watch out for evolution teachings in all of your science and social studies books and videos. I usually read the books beforehand, and skip over any material I do not agree with. Also, make sure your science lessons have your child see God's hand in nature. I recommend using Creation curriculum by Media Angels for a comprehensive unit study approach that is biblically based.

Computer Technology

Computer games, such as Knowledge Adventure's *Jumpstart World* and The Learning Company's *Oregon Trail* and *Carmen Sandiego* provide a hands-on approach to learning geography and history. Two educational websites that are very useful and deserve attention are *www.edhelper.com* and *www.enchantedlearning.com.* You have to become a member for a small annual fee to use the services, but they are well worth it. There are many other educational websites, but these have been the two that I consistently return to for ideas over the years. They are loaded with information and printable worksheets for every subject, holiday theme, and unit study you can think of. These are wonderful educational resources to have at your fingertips.

Useful Tips

- ☞ Children enjoy completing puzzles, so provide your child with puzzles of the world and the United States. Make it into a game by setting a timer and having your child play "Beat the Clock" by trying to complete the puzzle before the timer rings. I like to add a little extra competition for my oldest son, and we have a contest to see who can get the lowest time. This approach to learning geography is much more pleasurable than filling in the traditional outline maps.

- ☞ Play a license plate game as a family while traveling. The goal of this challenging game is to find all of the United States' license plates (excluding Hawaii and Alaska). Make your own outline map of the United States with the names of the states labeled, or print an outline map from the Internet. Place the U.S. map on a clipboard, and leave it in your car. Use a highlighter to shade in a state when your child sees the corresponding license plate. Work as a team to see how many states' license plates you can find.

☞ LeapFrog's Explorer is a talking globe that is fabulous for teaching geography. Children can point to different countries for information on their currency, population, area, current time, capital, and anthem. This talking globe also provides quizzes using geography questions.

☞ Have your child learn geography while he eats. Place a large map of an area your child is studying on your kitchen table. Cover it with a clear, plastic tablecloth. You can also purchase laminated placemats with maps on them.

☞ One fantastic method to use for studying history is to make timelines for historical events and biographies. This enables your child to visually comprehend the chronological order of events.

☞ Plan your family time around what your child is learning in school. Take a family vacation to Washington D.C. if your child is learning about U.S. history. Visit a planetarium if your child is learning about the solar system. Enjoy learning together as a family.

☞ An alternative to going on field trips is to take virtual field trips on-line. This saves you time and money by allowing your child to travel without leaving your home. One website that has a complete educational package with objectives, lesson plans, questions and answers, and sites to visit is *www.virtual-field-trips.com.*

☞ Life science should include live observations when applicable. Teach the process of metamorphosis with a butterfly or ladybug kit, and observe how the insects transform into beautiful works of God. Learn about plants by growing seeds in a garden. Discover the incredible life cycle of a frog by raising tadpoles.

Study the amazing underworld of insects through an ant farm. The idea is to allow your child to learn through observation. These are the science lessons children never forget.

☞ You may be able to order videos and books to correlate with what you are teaching from your library's on-line database. The library will call you when your books and/or videos arrive.

Board Games

Use educational board games to excite your child about learning. Snapshots Across America and Mad Dash! 3 Minutes Across America are excellent games for learning geography in a hands-on way. SomeBody is a fun board game for learning human anatomy. Your child can actually build a human body while learning interesting anatomy facts. Board games are especially terrific for kinesthetic learners.

Evaluation Methods

If you are wondering how to evaluate what your child has learned in these subject areas since there is usually not any formal testing in the unit studies approach, narration is the best proven technique. After your child hears or reads some information, have him give a verbal summary or draw a picture of what happened. Older children can write a summary. This evaluation process is a simple method that triggers both sides of the brain, and the results for long-term memory are astounding.

Another practical evaluation tool is a Know, Want, Learn (KWL) chart. Use this before and after a unit study in science and social studies. It is also helpful to use when reading informational books. To use a KWL chart, take a large sheet of paper or poster board, and divide it into three even sections. Label each section with these words.

KWL Chart

What I Know	What I Want to Know	What I Learned

Complete the first two sections before you begin a book or unit study, and fill in the last section after completing your research. I like using this technique because you can find out your child's background knowledge on a particular subject before you begin, your child has a purpose for learning during the unit study, and it makes a great evaluation tool of everything your child learned after he completes a unit study. Have fun making science and social studies come to life!

A Homeschooling Support Group

CHAPTER 7

♥♥

YOU NEED SUPPORT

And let us consider how we may spur one another on toward love and good deeds. Let us not give up meeting together, as some are in the habit of doing, but let us encourage one another- and all the more as you see the Day approaching.

~Hebrews 10:24-25

Homeschool support groups, also known as co-ops, are just as important as your curriculum and teaching style. These groups are essential for both the parent and the child. Your child desperately needs a sense of belonging, and you need positive encouragement.

Make it a priority.

This is an area parents often overlook because they are so focused on the academic part of homeschooling. The benefits of a support group are infinite. Your child needs opportunities to interact with other children to develop friendships. Your child also needs to be exposed to a healthy form of competition with his peers. In addition, some planned activities will enable your child to develop life skills.

I am fortunate to live in an area with many homeschooling support groups. The only downside to this is I have seen some parents who try to be involved in everything. Be selective and do not schedule too much. This will eventually lead to burnout in both you and your child.

Here are some options for locating a homeschool support group.

- ✓ Check with your local church.
- ✓ Do a search on-line.
- ✓ Ask fellow home educators.
- ✓ Contact your county's recreational facilities and community centers.
- ✓ Call your school district superintendent.
- ✓ Ask your local library.

If you are unable to find a support group in your area, why not organize one yourself? It is important for the group to be local for time-management purposes. Once your group is established, you may want to boost promotions with T-shirts or bumper stickers. Here are suggestions to advertise without spending money.

- ✓ Check out your own neighborhood and church for other homeschooling families.
- ✓ Try putting an ad in a local flyer or church newsletter.
- ✓ The library usually allows posting notices on a bulletin board or a resource area for flyers.
- ✓ Newspapers often feature a community bulletin board or calendar where they list upcoming events. Call your local papers and find out how they prefer to receive press releases, and submit the pertinent information about your first meeting or event to the editor a few weeks before your event.
- ✓ Your city may also have a community cable channel. Explain to the cable coordinator that your group is non-profit and new to the community. Request they post your press release on television for a week.

You can begin with just a couple of families, and you might be surprised at how fast a group can grow. I have been actively involved in a very large homeschool group (approximately 150 families) and a small homeschool group (20 families). Each type of group has its benefits.

Everyone gets involved.

Each parent needs to actively participate in the group. This means every parent should step up and be responsible for planning certain events, such as one school activity and field trip during the school year. Parents can share the responsibilities when coordinating larger events. Emails are an efficient means of communication rather than leaving messages or playing phone tag. Have your members check their email weekly to keep up-to-date on events.

It is nice for parents to get together on a regular basis without the children. You can have monthly planning sessions to put upcoming events on your school calendars. You can also have mini-workshops to share ideas on curriculum. (You can even bring this book. ☺) Sometimes going out to dinner with no agenda is a great way to get refreshed.

Have fun!

Your homeschool support group can have all the exciting activities that a school environment has, such as group events and field trips. You will have to establish deadlines for event sign-ups and require payment in advance if tickets are to be purchased. Here are some suggestions for group activities and field trips.

Group Events

art club
back-to-school party
Bible memory verse contest
career day
Christmas pageant
drama club
Easter party
end of the year party
family camping trip
foreign language club
game day
geography fair
parent dinner night
science fair
spelling bee
talent show
Thanksgiving party
Valentine's party

Field Trip Ideas

airport
animal shelter
aquarium
art gallery
bakery
bank
bowling alley
circus
farm
fire station
fudge shop
golf course
grocery store
ice cream parlor
military base
movie theater
museum
newspaper company
park
performing arts theater
phone company
police station
post office
power plant
radio station
recycling center
restaurant
skating rink
television station
theme parks
veterinarian office
water park
zoo

Field trips are important for children because they teach life skills, allow time for socialization, and are just plain fun! When planning field trips, ask for group rates and remind families about proper dress and punctuality. Have parents check their emails before leaving for field trips in case of last-minute changes, such as a "Plan B" due to poor weather conditions. Bring a thank you card the children can sign to present to the speaker, and encourage your children to use their manners.

My children receive more socialization from homeschool support groups than they would in a school setting. They get so excited to see their friends after they complete their school work. The best part is the other children are from families I know and share the same values with. Your homeschool support group can be the highlight of your school day!

I can't take it anymore! I want to put the kids in school, NOW!
Public or private?
Boarding!!

CHAPTER 8

♥♥♥

YOU CAN DO IT!

Yesterday is history.
Tomorrow is a mystery.
Today is a gift.
That's why we call it the present.

~Babatunde Olatunji

Every day is a gift, yet we all have days where we feel like we have fallen into a slump. Either our children are getting tired of the routine or we are. Maybe nothing seems to be going right, or distractions are more than usual. This chapter is designed to encourage and motivate you during those days.

Take breaks.

When you have hit "the wall," it is okay to take time off to regroup. This is a common feeling for any educator. Do not feel guilty or compelled to make up time later. Remember, school teachers have planning days to collect their thoughts, get caught up, and reenergize themselves.

I grant you full permission to cancel school for the day for an impromptu field trip, a visit with a relative, a volunteer day, or a picnic at the park on those days when the weather is picturesque.

When a "teachable moment" appears, drop your plans and grab the moment. This means producing an unplanned lesson on the spot when the door of opportunity opens to learning. This may be an area of extreme interest or an opportunity that won't last. For instance, your dog just had puppies, and you stop your original science plans to learn about caring for puppies. This spontaneity sparks the interest of the child and gives a different flavor to the meaning of learning.

If an opportunity comes to go on vacation or spend time with family, go for it! It does not matter if it falls outside your planned vacation time. That's the beauty of homeschooling! Your child will learn more in these days off than completing any assignment at home. These are the precious memories your child will carry in his heart for eternity.

Change is good.

Homeschooling constantly evolves with the changing needs of your child. If your school day is consistently not working out the way you planned, it may be time for some adjustments. Reevaluate your lesson plans and curriculum to determine if they are effectively meeting your goals. This may mean rearranging your schedule to accommodate your child's most attentive time of the day, adding a few more resources for a child struggling with a concept, or even revamping the whole program in a particular subject area.

I have made major changes many times in my homeschool curriculum. It is sometimes discouraging when this happens because I put a lot of time and energy into choosing materials. However, there are no guarantees, and change can be a positive experience for all. In fact, I sometimes ended up liking the changes better than my original plan.

The power of praise!

Your words have power. They affect your child's attitude and performance. Speak loving words that inspire and motivate your child to reach for new heights. Make your criticisms constructive and loving, and use enthusiasm when praising your child to encourage more success.

General praise is okay to use occasionally, but most praise should be specific when teaching. Always try to follow a simple phrase (general praise) with a detailed reason (specific praise). For example, "Fantastic! I like the way you _______________." Children need more than the occasional "good." There are several different ways to give general praise to your child on the following pages. These are great lists to refer back to occasionally. Remember to follow them with specific praise.

You did it!
That's great!
Clear, concise, and complete!
Very creative!
That's a well-developed theme.
Very interesting!
Fantastic!
That's really nice.
Your style has spark.
Your work has such personality.
That's clever.
That's very perceptive.
You're right on target.
I like the way you've handled this.
I like the way you're working.
Good thinking!
Your work has pizzazz.
A splendid job!
You're right on the mark.
Good reasoning!
Very fine work!
You figured it out.
Outstanding!
I appreciate your help.
Keep up the good work.
I'm so proud of you.
You've made my day.
This is a winner!
Perfect!
You're on the ball today.
Superb!
This is something special.
What a hard-worker!
That's quite an improvement.
Superior work!
Great going!
Much better!
Wait until ______sees this!
You're becoming an expert at this.
That's the right answer.
You're really moving on.

You're exactly right!
You're on the right track now.
What neat work!
Beautiful!
This is quite an accomplishment.
That's a good point.
You really outdid yourself today.
Super!
That's coming along nicely.
That's a very good observation.
Terrific!
This is prize-winning work.
Sensational!
I like your style.
Good for you!
You've really been paying attention.
You're really going to town.
That's an interesting point of view.
You've got it now.
You make it look so easy.
Nice going!
This shows you've been thinking.
Right on!
You've come a long way with this.
Top-notch work!
I appreciate your cooperation.
Marvelous!
This gets a five-star rating.
Excellent work!
Congratulations! You got ___ correct.
Magnificent!
WOW!
How impressive!
I commend you for your quick thinking.
Awesome!
The results were worth your hard work.
Nice Job!
I like the way you are working today.
Way to go!
I knew you could do it!

Reward your child.

Give your child incentives to work for during your school time. A wonderful technique is to set a small mason jar on the table during school time. Place one marble in the jar each time your child answers a problem or question correctly. You can add marbles for spelling words accurately, reading independently, writing sentences properly, and solving math problems. You can also add marbles for a positive attitude, neat handwriting, and good behavior.

Once your child has earned a marble, never remove it from the jar. When the jar is full, give your child a reward, such as a special dessert, a sticker, or a toy. Use your child's main love language (see p. 14) to help determine the best reward for your child. Younger children should be rewarded in a shorter time period than older children. Older children can have larger rewards to work towards, such as a trip to the movies or a sleepover with friends.

This is the recommended time frame to fill the jar if your child is working up to his full potential:

- Kindergarten- each session
- First and Second Grade- every two or three sessions
- Third and Fourth Grade- every five sessions
- Fifth and Sixth Grade- every ten sessions

There are variations to this technique. You can fill the jar with jelly beans, popcorn, or pennies. When the jar is filled with pennies, your child can trade them in for dollars for his reward if money motivates him.

You want your child to be excited about your school time together, so you can nurture his natural curiosity and desire to learn. This technique gives your child goals to work for, and it reinforces positive behavior.

Distractions galore, oh my!

When you have days that are filled with every distraction imaginable, your child can do independent learning activities, such as: reading, watching an educational video, completing math drills on the Math Shark, listening to books on tape, practicing musical instruments, playing learning games on the computer, or working on a project. You can set up an art station in one part of your house with construction paper, glue, markers, scissors, and other art supplies. If you have more than one child, have your children do buddy-up reading or play educational board games together.

The point is school does not need to stop just because you are temporarily busy. These are also fabulous ideas for those days you may not be feeling well, and there is no need for guilt because your child is still learning.

Get creative and switch things up.

If you sense yourself getting frustrated because your child is not grasping a particular concept, try teaching from a different angle. For example, if your child is struggling with the concept of time, think of ways to teach your child this concept that vary from the approach he is learning about time in his curriculum. Use a teaching clock. Play time match-up card games, time bingo, and time estimation games in the car. Ask your child questions throughout the day about time, such as "This casserole needs to cook for thirty-five minutes. What time will the oven timer ring?" Apply the concept you are teaching to real life.

A new approach to learning that takes advantage of today's technology is offered at *www.time4learning.com*. It is a convenient, on-line home education program that combines learning with fun, educational teaching games for a monthly fee. It has self-paced lessons with assessments in all subject areas. You can choose skills that your child is currently learning in his homeschool curriculum and reinforce them with this interactive technique using animated characters and games. I especially like using this program to extend difficult lessons for more practice and review in the summer.

Read the Word of God.

Whenever I begin to feel discouraged in life, I meditate on scriptures from the Bible. I put Bible verses in my daily planner, on the refrigerator, and in my dining room where my children complete their school work. I even have stenciled Bible verses on the walls around my home. God's words of encouragement always cheer me up. Here are some scriptures that have motivated me in my homeschool journey.

✞ Psalm 32:8
"I will instruct you and teach you in the way you should go;
I will counsel you and watch over you."

✞ Psalm 119:105
"Your Word is a lamp to my feet and a light for my path."

✞ Psalm 127:3-5
"Sons are a heritage from the Lord, children a reward from Him. Like arrows in the hands of a warrior are sons born in one's youth. Blessed is the man whose quiver is full of them."

✞ Psalm 143:10
"Teach me to do Your will, for you are my God; may Your good spirit lead me on level ground."

✞ Proverbs 2:6
"For the Lord gives wisdom, and from His mouth come knowledge and understanding."

✞ Proverbs 3:5-6
"Trust in the Lord with all your heart and lean not on your own understanding; in all your ways acknowledge Him, and He will make your paths straight."

✞ Proverbs 16:3
"Commit to the Lord whatever you do, and your plans will succeed."

✞ Proverbs 19:20
"Listen to advice and accept instruction, and in the end you will be wise."

✞ Proverbs 22:6
"Train a child in the way he should go, and when he is old he will not turn from it."

✞ Proverbs 23:12
"Apply your heart to instruction and your ears to words of knowledge."

✞ Matthew 6:34
"Therefore do not worry about tomorrow, for tomorrow will worry about itself. Each day has enough trouble of its own."

✞ Matthew 11:28-29
"Come to me all you who are weary and burdened, and I will give you rest. Take my yoke upon you and learn from me, for I am gentle and humble in heart, and you will find rest for your soul."

✞ John 14:27
"Peace I leave with you; my peace I give you. I do not give to you as the world gives. Do not let your hearts be troubled and do not be afraid."

✞ Galatians 5:22-23
"But the fruit of the Spirit is love, joy, peace, patience, kindness, goodness, faithfulness, gentleness and self-control. Against such things there is no law."

✞ 1 Corinthians 13
"Love is patient, love is kind. It does not envy, it does not boast, it is not proud. It is not rude, it is not self-seeking, it is not easily angered, it keeps no record of wrongs. Love does not delight in evil but rejoices with the truth. It always protects, always trusts, always hopes, always perseveres."

✞ Ephesians 3:20
"Now to Him who is able to do immeasurably more than all we ask or imagine, according to His power that is at work within us."

✞ Philippians 4:13
"I can do everything through Him who gives me strength."

Believe in yourself.

Some days you may second-guess yourself and feel like you are not "qualified" to teach your child. Let go of any negative thoughts concerning this. It is only the work of the enemy. Fear is Satan's number one weapon against home educators. You *are* the most capable person on earth to teach your child.

God chose you specifically to be your child's parent. It is a perfect combination only the Lord can arrange. You have been homeschooling your child since birth. You taught him to eat, walk, talk, pray, love, and get along with others. Nothing changes when your child reaches school age. You already taught your child the most important parts of life. The rest is just icing on the cake.

If I taught your child for one school day, one advantage there may be is the effectiveness of the methods and strategies I use, which are all listed in this book. On the other hand, there are many drawbacks of having me teach your child for one day instead of you. You know your child's strengths and weaknesses and when your child is working up to his full potential. You know his love languages, learning styles, and what skills he has already mastered. You know if something is bothering him emotionally and causing distractions. Most of all, you love your child unconditionally.

It amazes me that people ask how I can teach my own children. When I was a school teacher, I would have about thirty students with different backgrounds, interests, and abilities. It would take me most of a school year to really get to know my students. I finally would be making significant progress only to see them leave me at the end of the school year. I believe it is much easier teaching my own children, and I feel very blessed that God has given me the desire and opportunity to do so. Never second-guess your decision to have your child at home with you instead of in a classroom setting.

The lesson here is to see yourself as God sees you. God has put a desire in your heart to educate your child. Do not focus on your weaknesses; focus on your God. When God guides, He provides.

Hang in there on the tough days for there are brighter days around the corner. I know you can do it!

A reality TV show writers' meeting.

CHAPTER 9

♥♥

TLC'S TOP TEN FOR ODDS & ENDS

Education is simply the soul of a society as it passes from one generation to another.

~G. K. Chesterton

#10
Music Education

One of the best things you can give your child is the gift of music. Encourage your child to listen to and make music as early as possible. Your child can start by listening to his favorite songs and accompanying the music with simple instruments. He can later play more complex instruments and perhaps even take formal lessons.

Nancy Poffenberger's award winning books from Fun Publishing are perfect for parents who may not know music but want to teach their children the joy of music. These books are designed to be self-teaching and are so simplistic that my three and five-year-old sons are playing songs independently on the piano. The best part is I am learning to play instruments, too. I can finally play the piano for the first time in my life!

Learning to play music cultivates many skills that will continue to be useful to your child throughout his life. Playing a musical instrument will help your child develop concentration, patience, and perseverance. Practicing musical instruments will improve hand-eye coordination. The act of learning to play an instrument will build in your child a sense of pride and confidence. In addition, researchers have found a significant relationship between music instruction and positive performances in academic areas, such as: reading comprehension, spelling, mathematics, listening skills, motor skills, and primary mental abilities (verbal, perceptual, numeric, and spatial).

All in all, music has proven to provide more benefits to children than simple entertainment. Make it a priority to include music education in your school day.

#9
Foreign Language

Educators are becoming more aware of the advantages of learning a second language. In addition to developing a lifelong ability to communicate with more people, children may derive other benefits from early language instruction, including superior problem solving skills, an increased attention span, and greater cultural sensitivity.

The most entertaining Spanish program I have come across is *La Clase Divertida*, which translation means "The Fun Class." It is a complete Spanish curriculum for children from kindergarten through eighth grade designed by an elementary Spanish teacher. It uses a multi-sensory approach. It has cassettes, videos, workbooks, art projects with all the required materials, and recipes for cooking projects. I like how my son consistently hears the correct pronunciations that the instructors provide since I do not speak Spanish fluently. This hands-on approach to learning Spanish is a big hit with kids!

#8
Art Appreciation

I truly enjoy teaching art because children love to be imaginative. I have never been fond of the traditional art projects that you cut out the pattern, and glue the pieces together. Where's the creativity? I try to plan projects that allow room for originality, and I proudly display my children's work on our school's bulletin board- the refrigerator.

You must also teach methods and art history to the upper elementary grades. I usually alternate between a craft and a more structured art lesson every other week for the older children.

My top choice for introducing art concepts for third grade and up is *Drawing Basics* by Thomas Kinkade. The renowned artist designed this remarkable program, and he incorporates all the key elements of art as well as principles of design. The best part is the video-based instruction. This is especially helpful for parents who are not artistically talented. Your child can watch Thomas Kinkade draw, and replay the DVD if he needs to see it multiple times. It even has quizzes and tests to assess your child's learning.

My favorite art history program for upper elementary age children is *God and the History of Art* by Barry Stebbing. These art lessons teach the basic fundamentals in drawing, painting, and color theory while simultaneously teaching art history. It is a very thorough program that can be stretched over several years. Have fun getting the creative juices flowing!

#7
Elective Summer

Do you ever feel like there is not enough time to teach everything you want? One way of overcoming this is by having summer school. No, I'm not referring to year-round schooling or retention programs, but I'm suggesting an elective summer. You can designate different days or weeks for topics your child is interested in learning, such as: sewing, cooking, playing instruments, gardening, fishing, electronics, drawing, raising animals, and conducting science experiments.

This enables you to set aside time to address your family's interests that sometimes get skipped over during the busy school year. Continue reading aloud to your child, and encourage independent reading time during the summer. Check your local library for reading incentive programs offered in the summer months.

#6
Love to Learn

A must-have catalog for every homeschool parent is *Love to Learn*. This family-owned company sells a wide variety of educational merchandise at discounted prices. What sets this catalog apart from others is the mother's evaluation of the products. Diane Hopkins is a homeschooling mother who has taught all seven of her children. She has tested most of the products multiple times and gives a comprehensive review of them. Diane guided many of my decisions during my first few years of homeschooling through her helpful publications. I have purchased several Christmas and birthday gifts for my children from this catalog. Their products go well beyond academics. To be added to the mailing list, go to *www.lovetolearn.net*.

#5
Family Game Night

Some of the best memories with my children include family game night. One night a week we play board games together. The television is turned off, the housework is pushed aside, and my husband and I give our sons our undivided attention. I try to sneak in educational games, and each child takes a turn choosing a game. The educational games are probably not what you would expect. These are great items to put on your Christmas and birthday lists when friends and family need ideas for your child. There are many games available, but here are some of our family favorites:

- Hi Ho! Cherry-O, Connect Four, and Chutes and Ladders- counting skills for little ones
- Candy Land- color recognition for little ones
- Letter Getter and Scrabble Junior- phonics, spelling, and vocabulary
- Monopoly Junior, Pay Day, and The Game of Life- money skills
- Battleship- coordinate points for graphing
- Sorry, Trouble, Clue, Memory, Yahtzee, Uno, Checkers, Chinese Checkers, Chess, Mancala, Apples to Apples, and card games- critical thinking skills

You may already have many of these games but never realized your child was learning educational skills while playing them. Your child will also be learning how to follow rules, take turns, encourage one another, and have a positive attitude. Have fun making memories!

If you are unable to have a family game night, you can always invite some other homeschoolers over for a game day once a month. Get some pizza and sodas, and let the children bring their favorite games. Children can play board games for hours, and this surely beats playing video games. This is a social time homeschoolers truly enjoy.

#4
Assessment

When I worked as a homeschool evaluator, I would visit homes and assess children's learning. One common element I noticed was the overstuffed portfolio (and sometimes even more than one). A portfolio's purpose is to keep work "samples" of your child's progress, not everything he has worked on for the entire school year. It should consist of a few activities per month for each subject area. These quickly add up, and you will have a full, but not overstuffed, portfolio at the end of the school year. This process makes it much easier for a certified teacher to evaluate your child's progress, and it is more convenient for you to store for documentation purposes.

I use a three-ring binder with dividers for each subject. I save tests, quizzes, writing samples, and other evaluation methods. I also include certificates my child earned, special projects we worked on, and pictures of certain activities from our unit studies, such as experiments or field trips. These samples make up a well-rounded portfolio, which represents our school year.

Assessment usually goes hand-in-hand with grades. I have not seen any benefits of using grades in the elementary years. Do not give your child a low grade if he is working up to his full potential. Effort is what you want to assess, not intelligence. You know your child well enough to know if he is really trying. Since so much of the learning that takes place in these early years of education is developmental, why would you crush your child's spirit when he may be giving his best?

If your prefer using grades, your child does not need to know. You can grade your child's work samples before you insert them into his portfolio for recordkeeping purposes. This can be helpful for the end-of-the-year assessment, so the evaluator can quickly see if progress is being made. The goal in homeschooling is to learn the material, not grade the material and move on. For example, if my oldest son performs poorly for his ability on a spelling test, I will have him practice those words more and take the test again at a later time. I am more concerned about him learning the words than the test score. Focus on growing, not grading.

#3
Character Education

Character education needs to be specifically addressed as an integral component of a comprehensive education. Harvard and Stanford Universities have reported that the reason a person gets hired for a job and promoted in that job is due to eighty-five percent attitude and fifteen percent technical or specific skills. But, we often teach the opposite! This statistic makes it very clear that your child's character will matter more in life than his academic performance.

The goal of character education is to develop knowledge and life skills for responsible behavior. Problem solving, decision making, and conflict resolution are important parts of developing moral character. Through role-play and discussions, your child can see how his decisions affect other people and things. You can also guide your child toward television shows, movies, and books that portray positive values. Focus on the Family's *Adventures in Odyssey* series provides exciting movies, audio CDs, and books that concentrate on character-building traits. Here are some character traits and examples of classic stories that reflect them:

- Humility- *The Emperor's New Clothes*
- Wisdom-*King Midas*
- Perseverance- *The Tortoise and the Hare*
- Friendship- *The Four Musicians*
- Love- *Johnny Appleseed*
- Moderation- *The Fisherman and His Wife*
- Honesty- *The Honest Woodcutter*
- Generosity- *The Gift*
- Cooperation- *Stone Soup*
- Courage- *The North Wind*

If you concentrate on one character trait per month, you can cover all ten character traits in one school year. Your goal is to have your child display all of the character traits consistently.

#2
Schedule time for yourself.

Take time-outs. (I am talking about you and not your children.☺) Do not let homeschooling consume you. Parents often make their children their top priority and schedule little time for themselves. Trust me, I've been there. If you feel yourself getting stressed, take a break. You need to refresh and rejuvenate yourself.

Put exercise on the top of your "to-do" list, even if it is just a walk around your neighborhood. This is an excellent way to relieve stress. What about your hobbies? You are more than likely taking time for your child's extracurricular activities, so schedule time for things you enjoy, too.

Pamper yourself with a little indulgence. Do you like to get massages, facials, or manicures? Schedule these on your calendar ahead of time. If I do not put these things on my calendar, they do not happen. For special occasions, my husband purchases a few hours at a local spa for me. What a wonderful gift I truly enjoy- an afternoon of pure relaxation!

You deserve some "mom time." You can plan a night to scrapbook or watch a movie with other moms. Let the husbands baby-sit.

Try not to do everything. Stop trying to be "super mom" or "wonder woman." I am here to tell you it is okay to let go of that image. Enlist help from your spouse. Have your child complete chores around the house in the morning while you get organized for school. Pay someone to deep clean your house once a month. This is something I have begun because there never seemed to be enough time without children in my home to focus on monthly cleaning. Now I take my children somewhere for a few hours, and we return to a spotless house. What a great feeling!

#1
Make God your first priority.

Most importantly, include God every day in every way. The Bible identifies parents as children's most influential teachers. It commands parents to instruct their children when they walk, lay down, and get up. This means to consciously work at being your child's Christian educator.

Seize any opportunity to speak of God. Place a children's Bible where your child can read it. Around your home, place visible reminders that display your faith in God, such as Christian artwork and Bible verses. Give your child scriptures to memorize each week that relate to what he is learning at church or in his school lessons.

Your participation in church can create a desire to know God more intimately. Belonging to a church and creating a network of Christian friends gives children a sense of community. The Sunday school lessons, music, and pastor's sermons can stimulate interesting questions and conversations. I want my children to develop relationships with teachers, leaders, and mature Christians who can mentor them. There is much truth to the African proverb, "It takes a village to raise a child."

Ask God for wisdom and guidance when making decisions, such as curriculum choices and planning your school day. I have found the Holy Spirit to be a wonderful coordinator in my children's schooling.

Begin your school day with devotions and prayers by showing your child God always comes first. This goes for parents, too. Do not begin your day until you have had your Bible study and prayer time. Your relationship with God will be the most important thing you teach your child. I love the way Lisa Whelchel, from *Creative Correction*, affectionately says, "I would like my children to remember waking up every morning and peeking through the banisters to see me reading my Bible in my special chair, having a cup of coffee with Jesus and listening to what He wanted to tell me through His Word that day."

Wow! This is leaving a true and lasting legacy for our children. As parents, we need to create a thirst to know our Father and enjoy His love. It is God's desire to have a personal relationship with you. It is the reason that He created you. God gave each of us a will and freedom of choice. But we often choose to follow our own path, make our own way in life, or simply disobey God. This side of our human nature is called sin, and it separates us from God.

The Bible tells us that there is a solution to the problem of sin and separation from God. Because our heavenly Father loves us so much, He sent His son Jesus to die on the cross as a payment for our sins. Jesus took the penalty of our sin on Himself to bridge the gap between us and God. By acknowledging our sin and believing that Jesus paid the penalty for it once and for all, we can be forgiven and have the kind of relationship with God that will change our lives on earth and give us assurance of eternal life.

If you would like to commit or rededicate your life to God, pray this simple prayer, "Heavenly Father, I want to know You personally. I believe that You sent Your son, Jesus Christ, to take the punishment I deserve. You raised Him to life again, so I may have eternal life. I repent of my sins and thank You for Your forgiveness. I ask You to come into my heart. I make You my Lord and Savior. Take control of my life, and make me the kind of person You want me to be. In Jesus' name I pray, Amen."

Congratulations! You are born again if you have prayed this prayer. The angels are rejoicing in heaven. Here are some suggestions for your spiritual growth:

Go to God in prayer daily. (John 15:7)
Read God's Word daily. (Acts 17:11)
Obey God moment by moment. (John 14:21)
Witness for Christ with your words and actions. (Matthew 4:19)

Please visit *www.teachingwithtlc.com* if you would like more information on building your relationship with Christ.

That if you confess with your mouth, "Jesus is Lord," and believe in your heart that God raised him from the dead, you will be saved.

-Romans 10:9

Homeschooling requires devotion and commitment. There is no doubt about that. But the benefits are eternal. You are giving your child an education that is tailor-made just for him. You are instilling your values in him each day, and he will see your love in action. Your choice to educate at home is a gift of love. Be proud and thankful that you have the opportunity and freedom to provide that gift for your family.

I hope you find this guide helpful. I have sincerely enjoyed sharing my ideas and experiences with you. My wish is for your days to be filled with much love as you create memories that will last a lifetime. Remember successful teaching is not head-to-head; it is heart-to-heart.

Teacher's Prayer

I want to teach my children how
To live this life on earth,
To face its struggles and its strife
And to improve their worth.
Not just the lesson in a book
Or how the rivers flow,
But how to choose the proper path
Wherever they may go.
To understand eternal truth
And know right from wrong,
And gather all the beauty of
A flower and a song.
For if I help the world to grow
In wisdom and in grace,
Then I shall feel that I have won
And I have filled my place.
And so I ask Your guidance, God,
That I may do my part,
For character and confidence
And happiness of heart.

~James J. Metcalf

Newbery Medal Winners, Present–1922

2006: *Criss Cross* by Lynne Rae Perkins (Greenwillow Books/HarperCollins)
2005: *Kira-Kira* by Cynthia Kadohata (Atheneum Books for Young Readers/Simon & Schuster)
2004: *The Tale of Despereaux: Being the Story of a Mouse, a Princess, Some Soup, and a Spool of Thread* by Kate DiCamillo (Candlewick Press)
2003: *Crispin: The Cross of Lead* by Avi (Hyperion Books for Children)
2002: *A Single Shard* by Linda Sue Park (Clarion Books/Houghton Mifflin)
2001: *A Year Down Yonder* by Richard Peck (Dial)
2000: *Bud, Not Buddy* by Christopher Paul Curtis (Delacorte)
1999: *Holes* by Louis Sachar (Frances Foster)
1998: *Out of the Dust* by Karen Hesse (Scholastic)
1997: *The View from Saturday* by E.L. Konigsburg (Jean Karl/Atheneum)
1996: *The Midwife's Apprentice* by Karen Cushman (Clarion)
1995: *Walk Two Moons* by Sharon Creech (HarperCollins)
1994: *The Giver* by Lois Lowry (Houghton)
1993: *Missing May* by Cynthia Rylant (Jackson/Orchard)
1992: *Shiloh* by Phyllis Reynolds Naylor (Atheneum)
1991: *Maniac Magee* by Jerry Spinelli (Little, Brown)
1990: *Number the Stars* by Lois Lowry (Houghton)
1989: *Joyful Noise: Poems for Two Voices* by Paul Fleischman (Harper)
1988: *Lincoln: A Photobiography* by Russell Freedman (Clarion)
1987: *The Whipping Boy* by Sid Fleischman (Greenwillow)
1986: *Sarah, Plain and Tall* by Patricia MacLachlan (Harper)
1985: *The Hero and the Crown* by Robin McKinley (Greenwillow)
1984: *Dear Mr. Henshaw* by Beverly Cleary (Morrow)
1983: *Dicey's Song* by Cynthia Voigt (Atheneum)
1982: *A Visit to William Blake's Inn: Poems for Innocent and Experienced Travelers* by Nancy Willard (Harcourt)
1981: *Jacob Have I Loved* by Katherine Paterson (Crowell)
1980: *A Gathering of Days: A New England Girl's Journal, 1830-1832* by Joan W. Blos (Scribner)
1979: *The Westing Game* by Ellen Raskin (Dutton)

1978: *Bridge to Terabithia* by Katherine Paterson (Crowell)
1977: *Roll of Thunder, Hear My Cry* by Mildred D. Taylor (Dial)
1976: *The Grey King* by Susan Cooper (McElderry/Atheneum)
1975: *M. C. Higgins, the Great* by Virginia Hamilton (Macmillan)
1974: *The Slave Dancer* by Paula Fox (Bradbury)
1973: *Julie of the Wolves* by Jean Craighead George (Harper)
1972: *Mrs. Frisby and the Rats of NIMH* by Robert C. O'Brien (Atheneum)
1971: *Summer of the Swans* by Betsy Byars (Viking)
1970: *Sounder* by William H. Armstrong (Harper)
1969: *The High King* by Lloyd Alexander (Holt)
1968: *From the Mixed-Up Files of Mrs. Basil E. Frankweiler* by E.L. Konigsburg (Atheneum)
1967: *Up a Road Slowly* by Irene Hunt (Follett)
1966: *I, Juan de Pareja* by Elizabeth Borton de Trevino (Farrar)
1965: *Shadow of a Bull* by Maia Wojciechowska (Atheneum)
1964: *It's Like This, Cat* by Emily Neville (Harper)
1963: *A Wrinkle in Time* by Madeleine L'Engle (Farrar)
1962: *The Bronze Bow* by Elizabeth George Speare (Houghton)
1961: *Island of the Blue Dolphins* by Scott O'Dell (Houghton)
1960: *Onion John* by Joseph Krumgold (Crowell)
1959: *The Witch of Blackbird Pond* by Elizabeth George Speare (Houghton)
1958: *Rifles for Watie* by Harold Keith (Crowell)
1957: *Miracles on Maple Hill* by Virginia Sorenson (Harcourt)
1956: *Carry On, Mr. Bowditch* by Jean Lee Latham (Houghton)
1955: *The Wheel on the School* by Meindert DeJong (Harper)
1954: *...And Now Miguel* by Joseph Krumgold (Crowell)
1953: *Secret of the Andes* by Ann Nolan Clark (Viking)
1952: *Ginger Pye* by Eleanor Estes (Harcourt)
1951: *Amos Fortune, Free Man* by Elizabeth Yates (Dutton)
1950: *The Door in the Wall* by Marguerite de Angeli (Doubleday)
1949: *King of the Wind* by Marguerite Henry (Rand McNally)
1948: *The Twenty-One Balloons* by William Pène du Bois (Viking)
1947: *Miss Hickory* by Carolyn Sherwin Bailey (Viking)
1946: *Strawberry Girl* by Lois Lenski (Lippincott)
1945: *Rabbit Hill* by Robert Lawson (Viking)
1944: *Johnny Tremain* by Esther Forbes (Houghton)
1943: *Adam of the Road* by Elizabeth Janet Gray (Viking)

1942: *The Matchlock Gun* by Walter Edmonds (Dodd)
1941: *Call It Courage* by Armstrong Sperry (Macmillan)
1940: *Daniel Boone* by James Daugherty (Viking)
1939: *Thimble Summer* by Elizabeth Enright (Rinehart)
1938: *The White Stag* by Kate Seredy (Viking)
1937: *Roller Skates* by Ruth Sawyer (Viking)
1936: *Caddie Woodlawn* by Carol Ryrie Brink (Macmillan)
1935: *Dobry* by Monica Shannon (Viking)
1934: *Invincible Louisa: The Story of the Author of Little Women* by Cornelia Meigs (Little, Brown)
1933: *Young Fu of the Upper Yangtze* by Elizabeth Lewis (Winston)
1932: *Waterless Mountain* by Laura Adams Armer (Longmans)
1931: *The Cat Who Went to Heaven* by Elizabeth Coatsworth (Macmillan)
1930: *Hitty, Her First Hundred Years* by Rachel Field (Macmillan)
1929: *The Trumpeter of Krakow* by Eric P. Kelly (Macmillan)
1928: *Gay Neck, the Story of a Pigeon* by Dhan Gopal Mukerji (Dutton)
1927: *Smoky, the Cowhorse* by Will James (Scribner)
1926: *Shen of the Sea* by Arthur Bowie Chrisman (Dutton)
1925: *Tales from Silver Lands* by Charles Finger (Doubleday)
1924: *The Dark Frigate* by Charles Hawes (Little, Brown)
1923: *The Voyages of Doctor Dolittle* by Hugh Lofting (Lippincott)
1922: *The Story of Mankind* by Hendrik Willem van Loon (Liveright)

Caldecott Medal Winners, Present–1938

2006: *The Hello, Goodbye Window* illustrated by Chris Raschka; text by Norton Juster (Michael di Capua/Hyperion)
2005: *Kitten's First Full Moon* by Kevin Henkes (Greenwillow Books/HarperCollinsPublishers)
2004: *The Man Who Walked Between the Towers* by Mordicai Gerstein (Roaring Brook Press/Millbrook Press)
2003: *My Friend Rabbit* by Eric Rohmann (Roaring Brook Press/Millbrook Press)
2002: *The Three Pigs* by David Wiesner (Clarion/Houghton Mifflin)
2001: *So You Want to Be President?* illustrated by David Small; text by Judith St. George (Philomel Books)
2000: *Joseph Had a Little Overcoat* by Simms Taback (Viking)
1999: *Snowflake Bentley* illustrated by Mary Azarian; text by Jacqueline Briggs Martin (Houghton)
1998: *Rapunzel* by Paul O. Zelinsky (Dutton)
1997: *Golem* by David Wisniewski (Clarion)
1996: *Officer Buckle and Gloria* by Peggy Rathmann (Putnam)
1995: *Smoky Night* illustrated by David Diaz; text by Eve Bunting (Harcourt)
1994: *Grandfather's Journey* by Allen Say; text: edited by Walter Lorraine (Houghton)
1993: *Mirette on the High Wire* by Emily Arnold McCully (Putnam)
1992: *Tuesday* by David Wiesner (Clarion Books)
1991: *Black and White* by David Macaulay (Houghton)
1990: *Lon Po Po: A Red-Riding Hood Story from China* by Ed Young (Philomel)
1989: *Song and Dance Man* illustrated by Stephen Gammell; text: Karen Ackerman (Knopf)
1988: *Owl Moon* illustrated by John Schoenherr; text: Jane Yolen (Philomel)
1987: *Hey, Al* illustrated by Richard Egielski; text: Arthur Yorinks (Farrar)
1986: *The Polar Express* by Chris Van Allsburg (Houghton)
1985: *Saint George and the Dragon* illustrated by Trina Schart Hyman; text: retold by Margaret Hodges (Little, Brown)

1984: *The Glorious Flight: Across the Channel with Louis Bleriot* by Alice & Martin Provensen (Viking)
1983: *Shadow* translated and illustrated by Marcia Brown; original text in French: Blaise Cendrars (Scribner)
1982: *Jumanji* by Chris Van Allsburg (Houghton)
1981: *Fables* by Arnold Lobel (Harper)
1980: *Ox-Cart Man* illustrated by Barbara Cooney; text: Donald Hall (Viking)
1979: *The Girl Who Loved Wild Horses* by Paul Goble (Bradbury)
1978: *Noah's Ark* by Peter Spier (Doubleday)
1977: *Ashanti to Zulu: African Traditions* illustrated by Leo & Diane Dillon; text: Margaret Musgrove (Dial)
1976: *Why Mosquitoes Buzz in People's Ears* illustrated by Leo & Diane Dillon; text: retold by Verna Aardema (Dial)
1975: *Arrow to the Sun* by Gerald McDermott (Viking)
1974: *Duffy and the Devil* illustrated by Margot Zemach; retold by Harve Zemach (Farrar)
1973: *The Funny Little Woman* illustrated by Blair Lent; text: retold by Arlene Mosel (Dutton)
1972: *One Fine Day* retold and illustrated by Nonny Hogrogian (Macmillan)
1971: *A Story A Story* retold and illustrated by Gail E. Haley (Atheneum)
1970: *Sylvester and the Magic Pebble* by William Steig (Windmill Books)
1969: *The Fool of the World and the Flying Ship* illustrated by Uri Shulevitz; text: retold by Arthur Ransome (Farrar)
1968: *Drummer Hoff* illustrated by Ed Emberley; text: adapted by Barbara Emberley (Prentice-Hall)
1967: *Sam, Bangs & Moonshine* by Evaline Ness (Holt)
1966: *Always Room for One More* illustrated by Nonny Hogrogian; text: Sorche Nic Leodhas, pseud. [Leclair Alger] (Holt)
1965: *May I Bring a Friend?* illustrated by Beni Montresor; text: Beatrice Schenk de Regniers (Atheneum)
1964: *Where the Wild Things Are* by Maurice Sendak (Harper)
1963: *The Snowy Day* by Ezra Jack Keats (Viking)
1962: *Once a Mouse* retold and illustrated by Marcia Brown (Scribner)
1961: *Baboushka and the Three Kings* illustrated by Nicolas Sidjakov; text: Ruth Robbins (Parnassus)

1960: *Nine Days to Christmas* illustrated by Marie Hall Ets; text: Marie Hall Ets and Aurora Labastida (Viking)
1959: *Chanticleer and the Fox* illustrated by Barbara Cooney; text: adapted from Chaucer's Canterbury Tales by Barbara Cooney (Crowell)
1958: *Time of Wonder* by Robert McCloskey (Viking)
1957: *A Tree Is Nice* illustrated by Marc Simont; text: Janice Udry (Harper)
1956: *Frog Went A-Courtin'* illustrated by Feodor Rojankovsky; text: retold by John Langstaff (Harcourt)
1955: *Cinderella, or the Little Glass Slipper* illustrated by Marcia Brown; text: translated from Charles Perrault by Marcia Brown (Scribner)
1954: *Madeline's Rescue* by Ludwig Bemelmans (Viking)
1953: *The Biggest Bear* by Lynd Ward (Houghton)
1952: *Finders Keepers* illustrated by Nicolas, pseud. (Nicholas Mordvinoff); text: Will, pseud. [William Lipkind] (Harcourt)
1951: *The Egg Tree* by Katherine Milhous (Scribner)
1950: *Song of the Swallows* by Leo Politi (Scribner)
1949: *The Big Snow* by Berta & Elmer Hader (Macmillan)
1948: *White Snow, Bright Snow* illustrated by Roger Duvoisin; text: Alvin Tresselt (Lothrop)
1947: *The Little Island* illustrated by Leonard Weisgard; text: Golden MacDonald, pseud. [Margaret Wise Brown] (Doubleday)
1946: *The Rooster Crows* by Maude & Miska Petersham (Macmillan)
1945: *Prayer for a Child* illustrated by Elizabeth Orton Jones; text: Rachel Field (Macmillan)
1944: *Many Moons* illustrated by Louis Slobodkin; text: James Thurber (Harcourt)
1943: *The Little House* by Virginia Lee Burton (Houghton)
1942: *Make Way for Ducklings* by Robert McCloskey (Viking)
1941: *They Were Strong and Good* by Robert Lawson (Viking)
1940: *Abraham Lincoln* by Ingri & Edgar Parin d'Aulaire (Doubleday)
1939: *Mei Li* by Thomas Handforth (Doubleday)
1938: *Animals of the Bible, A Picture Book* illustrated by Dorothy P. Lathrop; text: selected by Helen Dean Fish (Lippincott)

HELPING TO LAY THE FOUNDATION FOR TOMORROW'S GENERATION

Please visit us on-line at
www.teachingwithtlc.com
for teaching tips and educational products.